SECRET
MADRID

Verónica Ramírez Muro

With the special collaboration of Natalia Pianzola

Photos: Manuel Vázquez

Jonglez

We have taken great pleasure in drawing up
Secret Madrid and hope that through its guidance
you will, like us, continue to discover unusual,
hidden or little-known aspects of the city.
Descriptions of certain places are accompanied
by thematic sections highlighting historical details
or anecdotes as an aid to understanding the city in
all its complexity.
Secret Madrid also draws attention to the multitude
of details found in places that we may pass every
day without noticing. These are an invitation to
look more closely at the urban landscape and,
more generally, a means of seeing our own city
with the curiosity and attention that we often
display while travelling elsewhere …

Comments on this guidebook and its contents,
as well as information on places we may not have
mentioned, are more than welcome and will enrich
future editions.

Don't hesitate to contact us:
• Éditions Jonglez, 17, boulevard du Roi,
  78000 Versailles, France
• E-mail: info@jonglezpublishing.com

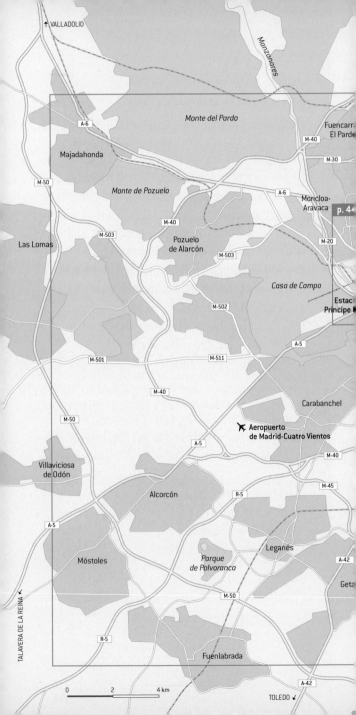

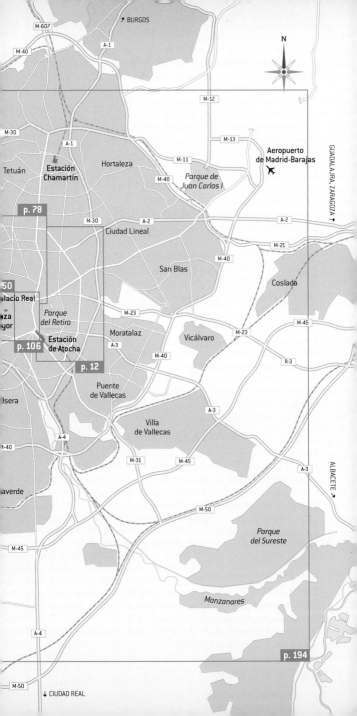

CONTENTS

NORTH

CENTRE-EAST

CONTENTS

CENTRE-WEST

CONTENTS

FARTHER AWAY

INDEX

EAST

COLONIA MADRID MODERNO

La Guindalera district
Calles Castelar, Cardenal Beluga and Roma; Avenues Toreros, Cartagena,
Francisco Navacerrada, Campañar and Ruiz Perelló
• Metro: Ventas

A trip through time

A walk around the streets of La Guindalera district is like going back in time. The houses are detached and some of them, such as those in Calles Roma and Cardenal Beluga, are neo-Mudejar in style.

This district was at least twenty-five years in construction, with the first phase of the project dating from 1890. The third and last phase, in Art Nouveau style, was carried out in 1905 by architect Valentín Roca Carbonell. The initiative for this project, known as Madrid Moderno, goes back to architect Julián Marín, but following legal problems the work was delayed for years, leading to a real architectural hotchpotch.

The houses are laid out in rows. Those of the first phase have circular neo-Mudejar towers, with a small garden and a brick and *azulejo* façade. The remainder, on the other hand, show no homogeneity, which led to numerous criticisms pointing out the poor taste and random planning of the district. However, a century later, the houses that are still standing, such as those of Calle Castelar, known as "Calle de los Hotelitos" ("Street of the Little Villas"), retain a certain charm. Unfortunately, many of them have succumbed to pressure from property developers.

MADRID DESDE TORRES BLANCAS

The Torres Blancas building (No. 37 Avenida de América – Metro: Avenida de América) is noteworthy not only for its architecture but because it provided the subject matter for the painting *Madrid desde Torres Blancas* (Madrid seen from Torres Blancas) by Antonio Lopez, which was sold at auction in 2008 for 1.5 million euros, the highest price ever paid for a contemporary Spanish artist. In the painting, Lopez immortalises the view of Madrid which the inhabitants of the "white towers" enjoy every day.

Although the structure is in fact grey, it is called Las Torres Blancas because the initial project envisaged the two tower blocks being built in white marble. However, funds for the project were insufficient and the building was left incomplete, in spite of the commitment of Juan Huarte, a Spanish entrepreneur and patron of the arts who wanted a building that broke with the architectural language of the day. In 1961 the project was offered to the architect Francisco Javier Sáezn de Oiza, who created a skyscraper of organic form. In effect, the 21-floor building resembles a giant tree, with foliage overflowing from balconies placed along the trunk and the summit occupied by circular terraces.

ROYAL BAPTISMAL FONT

Monasterio de Santo Domingo el Real
Calle de Claudio Coello, 112
• Tel: 91 563 55 42
• Suggested visiting times to avoid interrupting Mass: from 10am to
12pm and 4pm to 6pm
Admission free
Metro: Núñez de Balboa

> *Font where
> St Dominic
> was baptised?*

The font in which it is thought St Dominic de Guzmán was baptised in 1170 is the very one used by the royal household to baptise the heirs to the Spanish crown. It is at present in the care of the Dominican Sisters of Santo Domingo el Real, in Salamanca district. This sober and austere red-brick edifice includes a niche reserved for the font, reached from the right-hand side of the church, where it is kept until needed for a royal baptism.

The tradition of this sacred font goes back to the seventeenth century, when Philip III took it to Valladolid to baptise his son Philip IV. On learning of the canonisation of St Dominic de Guzmán in 1234, Ferdinand III (San Fernando) had qualified the font as "Royal" and decreed that it should only be used for heirs to the crown.

This relic was among a few artefacts that survived the pillage of the first Santo Domingo monastery, built in 1218 on the square named after the saint in the centre of Madrid. When it was demolished following the damaged inflicted during the War of Independence (1808) and the 1868–1873 revolution ("*La Gloriosa*"), the font was installed in a new building in Calle de Claudio Coello.

The font is a block of white stone from Roman times, enhanced with gold and silver, bearing the emblems of the Dominican Order and the royal coat of arms. It was recoated with silver in 1771: 174 ounces (around 6 kilos) of metal were required.

As the font was reserved for royal usage it was not returned to Caleruega (Burgos), birthplace of the saint, but was kept in Madrid on the orders of Ferdinand III, first in the original monastery then in Santo Domingo el Real, where it remains to this day.

The font has only been taken from its niche for royal sacraments, but it has nevertheless travelled to Valladolid, Seville, La Granja (Segovia), El Pardo, the Palacio Real and the Palacio de la Zarzuela.

Its most recent trips were for the baptism of Leonor and Sofía, daughters of Spanish Crown Prince Philip of Asturias and his wife Princess Letizia. All documentation relating to these movements is recorded in the monastery registry.

King Juan Carlos was not baptised in this font, as in his early years the royal family was in exile at Rome.

CORNICE OF BUILDING ON CALLE DE CLAUDIO COELLO

Calle de Claudio Coello, 104
• Metro: Rubén Darío

> **Explosion that catapulted Carrero Blanco's car over a five-storey building**

At No. 104 Calle de Claudio Coello, a plaque commemorates the assassination on 20 December 1973, of Admiral Luis Carrero Blanco, prime minister and designated successor of the ageing Franco.

That morning, Carrero Blanco had attended Mass, as he did every day, at the Jesuit church in Calle Serrano. There was nothing to raise suspicions that the man who followed him at the communion rail was Arriaga, an ETA member who had been planning the assassination for months.

On Carrero Blanco's return from Mass, driving along Claudio Coello, his vehicle was blown up.

Cracks in the road surface are a reminder of the hole made by the explosion, which catapulted the car over a five-storey building to land in a courtyard on the other side. You can still see the damage to the cornice of the building where the car struck it, and the basement window from where ETA members excavated a tunnel out to the middle of the road. There they placed 100 kilos of explosives which caused the death of Carrero Blanco, his bodyguard and his driver. The basement had been rented by a so-called sculptor, which justified the noise of the pneumatic drill used to excavate the tunnel where the bomb would be placed, as well as the comings and goings of workers carrying

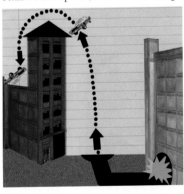

sacks of sand, without arousing the neighbours' suspicions. *"Operación Ogro"* (*"Operation Ogre"*) was the code name used during the planning of this assassination. As the United States Embassy wasn't far away, it was at first thought that the CIA may have been involved, but ETA claimed responsibility for the attack, which changed the Spanish political landscape.

RUBENS AT THE FUNDACIÓN CARLOS DE AMBERES

Calle de Claudio Coello, 99
- Tel. 91 435 22 01
- Open Monday–Friday from 9am to 2pm and 5pm to 8pm
- Metro: Núñez de Balboa

A little-known Rubens in San Andrés de los Flamencos chapel

The masterpiece *El martirio de san Andrés* (*The Martyrdom of St Andrew*) by Baroque artist Peter Paul Rubens is preserved at the Fundación Carlos de Amberes (Charles of Antwerp Foundation), which even local residents are unfamiliar with. The history of this institution began in 1594 when Carlos de Amberes ceded various buildings on Calle San Marcos to set up a hospice to take in pilgrims and local residents originating from what was then the Spanish Netherlands. Hence was born the hospital of San Andrés de los Flamencos and its chapel in 1606. The original building was destroyed in 1848 and a new one constructed on its present site in 1877. Today, the two pavilions of the former hospital are given over to cultural activities.

The church, in the form of a Latin cross with a vaulted nave, is itself used as an exhibition space. You can still see the jube and the site of the former high altar where Rubens' magnificent painting is hanging, still in its original frame made by the ebonists Abraham Lers and Julien Beymar, who were in the service of Philip IV. The result of a commission made in 1635 through the agency of the Palatine Printers of Antwerp, one of the benefactors of the institution, this treasure graces the high altar of San Andrés de los Flamencos chapel.

The painting, from the last period of the Flemish painter's work, shows a dramatic scene from the St Andrew's martyrdom, as described in the *Legenda aurea* (*Golden Legend*), a medieval collection of hagiographies by Jacobus de Voragine. The saint is shown about to be crucified on an X-shaped cross as the soldiers are binding him, while two women beg for mercy at his feet and another soldier designates the martyr. According to Jacobus, Andrew refused to be freed and pronounced the following words: "Why have you come? If it's to ask for pardon, you shall have it, but if it's to release me and free me, don't waste your time, it's too late …" The colours, the lighting and the facial expressions unite to create a work of great beauty.

This Foundation, one of the oldest private European non-profit institutions, encourages cultural exchanges with the former provinces of Flanders, organising exhibitions, classical music and jazz concerts, as well as producing publications. Since Philip III agreed to be patron of the institution at the beginning of the seventeenth century, this responsibility has traditionally been transferred to the reigning Spanish monarch.

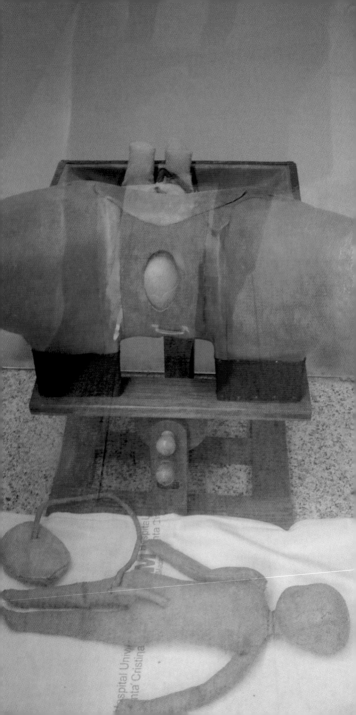

PRIVATE COLLECTION OF THE FORMER MIDWIVES SCHOOL

⑤

Escuela de Matronas y Casa de Salud
Hospital Santa Cristina
Calle Maestro Vives, 2
• Metro: O´Donnell
• Request permission to visit in the entrance hall

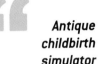

Antique childbirth simulator

Visitors hungry for scientific curiosities should stop off at Santa Cristina hospital, which houses an unusual collection of surgical instruments and memorabilia from the former Midwives School. In a glass case you can see forceps, pliers and pincers of the period, as well as a device that simulates the dilation of the cervix and recreates a delivery, with a doll taking the place of the newborn. There are also dossiers on the midwives who assisted women at their homes, because at the time it was common to give birth at home. For this reason, Alfonso XIII and Queen Maria Christina encouraged the construction of a specialist maternity centre and a school for the professional training of midwives. The queen then urged local noblewomen to have their babies delivered in this centre so that other women would follow their example.

The hospital was built between 1904 and 1924 by Luis Landecho and Jordán de Urríes, who designed a structure divided into four pavilions that could accommodate an average of 1,000 women per year, and provided lodgings, work and study space for the midwives.

NEARBY

LA CASA DE LAS ABEJAS

⑥

At No. 47 Calle del Doctor Esquerdo, the building is known as "Casa de las Abejas" (House of the Bees) because of the swarm of bees leaving the hive that decorates the façade. This very striking frontage belongs to La Moderna Apicultura (Modern Apiculture), a shop founded in 1925, at a time when "modern" meant the modernist architectural movement (Art Nouveau) then in vogue. The construction, which began in 1919 at the request of Antonio Garay Vitorica, was overseen by the architect Secundino Zuazo. La Moderna Apicultura was the first commercial honey manufacturer in Spain and supplied the royal household. In time, the original establishment closed its doors and now there only remains the shop where honey is filtered and packaged. It has kept some of the original fittings and notably the artisanal method of preparing the different varieties of honey sold there (over twenty).

PRIVATE VISIT TO THE BIBLIOTECA NACIONAL ❼ DE ESPAÑA

Paseo de Recoletos, 20
- Tel: 91 580 77 59
- Visits Friday at 5pm
- Open Day around 23 April
- Metro: Colón

Exceptional research library

At 5pm on Fridays, by booking in advance, you can visit the Biblioteca Nacional de España (National Library of Spain), normally only open to members and researchers. The tour of this monumental structure, built in 1866 by Francisco Jareño, begins opposite the symbolic statue of Alfonso X "El Sabio" ("The Wise"), with an explanation of the history of the site.

Officially, the National Library opened its doors on 16 March 1896, although as long ago as 1712 Philip V had decreed royal privilege, enabling each work to be secured for posterity. This privilege, which is really the predecessor of copyright registration, obliged printers to deposit a copy of all books printed in Spain so that they could be kept in the Public Library of the palace. The name was changed in 1836 to the National Library.

The tour continues in the library's museum on the ground floor. It lasts about an hour and a half, and you can learn about the history of book production from the first printing presses. Next comes a mention of the bibliographical treasures preserved by the library, such as the *Metz Codex*, a ninth-century manuscript which is at once an astronomical calendar, a manual of calculations and a treatise on astronomy. You can also see a copy

of the *Catholicon*, a Latin dictionary by Johannes Balbus printed in 1460, probably at Gutenberg.

Finally, through a series of videos, images and artefacts, visitors can gain a fair idea of the work that goes on in a library, the classification and storage systems for the 20 million books in the collection, and changes in techniques over the years.

Special rooms for conserving manuscripts, incunabula, plans and codices can only be visited if you have some justification for doing so, such as a link with the world of books (professional, student or collector).

Around 23 April, an open day is organised during which you can make a complete tour of the facilities.

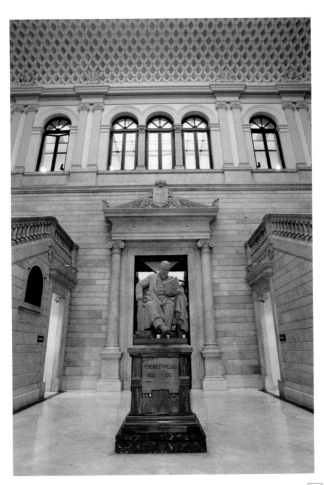

HIDDEN SYMBOLISM OF FUENTE DE CIBELES ❽

Plaza de Cibeles
• Metro: Banco de España

Relationship between Cybele and the bear on Madrid's coat of arms

Cybele was a Phrygian goddess also known as the Great Mother of the Gods. She represented fertility and nature. Her cult, which grew up in Asia Minor and spread throughout Ancient Greece under the name Potnia Theron (Mistress of the Animals), reached Rome around 204 BC. She was considered as the divinity of the life-death-rebirth cycle because of the resurrection of the fertility demi-god Attis, her supposed lover. Attis is also linked to the rite of the bloody execution of a bull, the symbol of fecundity in nature, a sort of "divinity sacrificed by the hand of man".

According to Greek mythology, the goddess was the incarnation of Gaia or Mother Earth, the embodiment of nature.

Often shown astride a chariot drawn by lions, her cult was originally a strict celebration of fertility which later diverged into orgiastic happenings.

Cybele is thus the goddess of the Earth, daughter of the Heavens, spouse of Saturn, mother of Jupiter, Pluto and Neptune (whose fountain, originally built opposite Cybele's, was later dismantled and moved to Plaza Cánovas del Castillo). She is the symbol of the vital energy concentrated in the Earth. She gave birth to the four natural elements (air, fire, water, earth) and represents the primary source of all fecundity.

The fact that her chariot is drawn by lions indicates that she dominates,

orders and directs the vital force. She repeatedly appears surmounting a wall (signifying the *genius loci* or "guardian spirit of the place", a cult established by the Romans) and is crowned with a seven-branched star or with a crescent moon, signs of her power over the cycles of biological evolution on Earth.

The moon symbol associates Cybele with the night star, which is itself linked to the bear, the main figure on Madrid's coat of arms. A bear was also to be found in the plaza until 1895, the year when the fountain (built by Ventura Rodriguez between 1777 and 1782) underwent major restoration, which changed its original appearance. Greek

mythology has it that the moon goddess frequently appeared as a bear, or a she-bear, when she took part in the rites to celebrate the fertility of Mother Earth, thanks to the undulating terrestrial currents represented in this same fountain by the image of a serpent.

The transformation of Cybele into a bear signifies that the goddess is the sovereign mother of all the material powers of the world, which is why the Romans worshipped her in the form of a square black stone, which evolved into a wheeled chariot, the very symbol of Mother Earth's own evolution.

On the original statue of the Madrid Cybele you could also see a stone griffin. The presence of this fantastical animal with the beak and wings of an eagle and the body of a lion expresses the Cybeline duality of human and divine nature, as mother of the Earth and daughter of the Heavens. It also associates the earthly power of the lion with the celestial energy of the eagle and thus forms part of the general symbolism of the forces of redemption, which also invoke the dual divine condition of strength and wisdom. In this fountain, wisdom is represented by Cybele's sceptre and the key she holds in her hand.

The black stone, as well as the solar team drawing Cybele's chariot (the lion symbolising the Sun) are probably also linked to the Black Stone of Islam (Kaaba), the Merkabah (throne or chariot of Judaic tradition), and even with the Cornerstone of Christian temples.

Modern bullfights are deeply rooted in the ancestral rite of the bloody execution of a bull associated with Attis, Cybele's lover.

CAÑADA
DE
7520 M.

BOUNDARY STONE IN PLAZA DE LA INDEPENDENCIA

9

• Metro: Retiro

Reminder of the flocks' passage

In Plaza de la Independencia, not far from the entrance to Buen Retiro gardens, is a boundary stone bearing the inscription "Cañada 7523 M".

The significance of this inscription goes back to the reign of the Visigothic King Euric (415–484), who decreed the first arrangements for the movement of livestock when Madrid and its surroundings were still fields. In the Middle Ages, Alfonso X accorded a number of privileges to the shepherds, such as exemption from military service or acting as a trial witness, and regulated the routes and tracks that allowed the passage of flocks of sheep during transhumance (see box). Formerly, the animals entered the city by Calle de Alcalá, and even through Puerta de Alcalá, which is why the track still retains the title of *cañada real*,* hence the stone inscription: Cañada and the number 7523 M, indicating the width of this particular route.

One of the functions of the boundary stones lining the *cañada real* was to define the route so that no property or construction encroached upon this 75 metre space to let the animals pass through freely. Sadly, most of the *cañadas reales* gradually fell into disuse because of the growth of towns and the feeding of livestock on commercial fodder instead of a more natural diet.

Transhumance began after the shearing, in May, and carried on until the following month. The distance covered varied around 20 kilometres a day. The only restrictions on the shepherds were to avoid village pastures, crops, vineyards, wheatfields and vegetable plots.

With time, this traditional usage has practically disappeared, although many of the *cañadas* have been rescued by mountain-bike riders and ramblers who like to be near to nature.

SHEEP IN TOWN

In an event that first took place in 1994, every year on the last Sunday of October around a thousand sheep invade the centre of Madrid, much to the astonishment of locals and tourists alike. The streets of the capital are closed to traffic so that the flock can make its way unimpaired from Casa de Campo to Plaza de Cibeles. What happens in the countryside is thus reproduced in a city setting: transhumance, or the herding of flocks from high-altitude summer pastures to lower winter grazing. Such migrations have been taking place for centuries along the *cañadas reales*.

Cañada real: a network of tracks for moving livestock on a seasonal basis (transhumance).

HINGES OF THE PUERTA DE ALCALÁ

Although now a ceremonial monument, Puerta de Alcalá was once a gateway, and was used as such until 1869. At the time there was a metal barrier, and some of the hinges that allowed it to be opened and closed can still be seen. During the day the gate was open, but it was closed at night for security.

Former gateway to the city

WHY ARE THE TWO SIDES OF PUERTA DE ALCALÁ DIFFERENT?

A special feature of Puerta de Alcalá escapes the attention even of those who have studied it carefully: the east face is nothing like the west face, and the reason for this is a misunderstanding between Charles III and the architect Francisco Sabatini.

In 1769, Charles III, who found the original gate insufficiently majestic for his taste, commissioned a new one and called for architects. Three responded: Ventura Rodríguez presented five projects, José de Hermosilla one, and the Italian Francisco Sabatini made two proposals inspired by Roman Baroque architecture.

Sabatini was commissioned and construction began in 1776 and finished two years later. But as the king had been enthusiastic about both projects and Sabatini was unsure which had been chosen, he decided to incorporate the two designs. So, whereas the east face has ten granite columns, the west has six (the others are pillars).

The sculptures surmounting them are also quite different: on the east side there are statues whereas on the west there are shields. The foremost sculptors of the age were called upon to complete the details: Francisco Gutiérrez and Roberto Michel. They were commissioned for the lions (evoking royalty), the horns (symbol of prosperity and abundance), the royal coat of arms supported by allegories of fame and a demi-god, and finally the children on the cornice (representing the four virtues of Strength, Temperance, Justice and Prudence).

WATERWHEEL OF THE REAL FÁBRICA DE PORCELANA DEL BUEN RETIRO

❶❶

Paseo Duque de Fernán Núñez
Between La Glorieta and Puerta del Ángel Caído
• Metro: Retiro

> *Wooden waterwheel dating from 1760*

In a corner of the Retiro district rests an old wooden *noria** which now serves as a reminder of the Real Fábrica de Porcelana (Royal Porcelain Factory) of Buen Retiro, popularly known as "La China". This type of waterwheel is called a *noria "de tiro"* (draft) or *"de sangre"* (blood), as it required the strength of an animal to raise the water that fed the former factory. The *noria* is the last vestige of the vast factory, discovered during an archaeological dig almost two hundred years after it closed, in fact after its destruction during the War of Independence.

La Real Fábrica de Porcelana was built on the order of Charles III in 1760 and work was carried out in the strictest secrecy so that nobody could discover how the magnificent pieces were manufactured. Charles III brought back a range of formulae from Italy (Capodimonte): while he reigned over Naples and Sicily he developed a real passion for porcelain.

Before this, porcelain had been imported from China, where manufacturing secrets were jealously guarded. At the beginning of the 18th century, Augustus III (Elector of Saxony and King of Poland) funded the creation of the first porcelain factory in Europe, at Meissen. The Sèvres factory in France and Wedgwood in England followed. Augustus III was Charles III's father-in-law, and his passion for porcelain was born after he was presented with a Grünes Watteau breakfast set that sported, on each piece with its pastoral motifs, the arms of the Kingdom of the Two Sicilies and those of Poland-Saxony. This encouraged Charles III to have his own factory built in 1743, first at Capodimonte then Madrid, on the site where the Fallen Angel statue now stands (see p. 35-37). During all these years, the ongoing research into the secrets of hard-paste porcelain, like that made at Meissen, grew into a real obsession. For the first five years, the factory produced a series of pieces of Chinese inspiration to decorate the porcelain room at the Palacio Real, Aranjuez.

In later years, the subjects changed according to the creative team at work. The majority of the pieces were sent to the Palacio Real, the Casita del Príncipe and El Escorial monastery. They are all now considered as genuine treasures.

---

*Noria: water-powered scoop wheel to raise water in buckets or clay pots.

UNRECOGNISED SYMBOLISM
OF THE MONUMENT DEDICATED TO LUCIFER

⑫

Buen Retiro gardens
• Metro: Retiro

> *666:*
> *the number*
> *of the Beast*
> *of the Apocalypse*

The statue of Lucifer in Buen Retiro gardens was the first in the world dedicated to this accursed angel, who rebelled against the will of God and was eternally damned.

This 1877 work is by the Madrid sculptor Ricardo Bellver (main statue) and Francisco Jareño (pedestal). Bellver's design was inspired by Book I of John Milton's epic poem *Paradise Lost:* "… his pride had cast him out from Heaven, with all his host of rebel angels … round he throws his baleful eyes that witnessed huge affliction and dismay mixed with obdurate pride and steadfast hate".

The site of Lucifer's statue is 666 metres above sea-level at Alicante, an astonishing fact as the altitude of the Spanish capital is 665 metres from that reference point. Considering that the Apocalypse of St John the Apostle (Book of Revelation) declares 666 to be the number of the Beast, it might well be asked how the city of Madrid accepted a statue carrying such a negative connotation.

In fact, 666 is also the number of the creation and evolution of man in nature, the one who is born after a cycle of nine months, the exact addition and reduction of this apocalyptic number (6+6+6=18 and 1+8=9).

It was also long thought, and some still believe (see below) that the Fall does not only carry negative connotations: it is no accident that the statue shows a serpent entwined around the Fallen Angel. The serpent does sometimes represent wisdom, as claimed by the apostle Matthew (10:16): "… wise as serpents, and harmless as doves".

Lucifer can thus also be seen as he who brings light to the world, as shown by the etymology of his name (from the Latin *lux fero:* light bearer) although he is bound with chains to his destiny and to the rocks, as seen at the base of the statue.

LUCIFER: MORE THAN A DEVIL ANGEL, A FALLEN ANGEL WHO CARRIES THE LIGHT TO SAVE HUMANITY?

For the Romans, Lucifer represented the morning star (*stella matutina*) and the evening star (*stella vespertina*).

It is also by this name that we know the planet Venus, the last to disappear before dawn and the first to appear at twilight (Venus is the third brightest object in the sky, after the Sun and moon).

In the Old Testament (according to Father Antonio Figueiredo who translated the Bible into Portuguese), Lucifer is only mentioned in Isaiah (14:12): "How art thou fallen from heaven, O Lucifer, son of the morning ...". However some maintain that this is a translation error.

In the Vulgate (Latin) Bible, the name of Lucifer appears six times, and always in reference to the morning star, as for example, in Peter (1:19): "Moreover, we possess the prophetic word as an altogether reliable thing. You do well if you pay attention to this as you would to a light shining in a murky place, until the day dawns and the morning star rises in your hearts."

In Revelation (22:16), Jesus also appears as the morning star, as in the early years of Christianity Jesus was referred to as Lucifer.

The name of Lucifer was thus common among the first Christians, as in the case of St Lucifer of Cagliari, bishop of Sardinia, who died between 370 and 371, and whose feast day is celebrated by the Church of Cagliari on 20 May.

It was the Book of Enoch, a second-century apocryphal text, which started the myth of fallen angels. In this text, Lucifer, the best-looking and best-loved of God's angels, was expelled from the Heavenly throne and fell to Earth. Lucifer (also called Luzbel) refused to obey the command of God to create a material being, Man. He thought that such a creation was unworthy and in contradiction to his divine state. So God sent the Archangel Michael, chief of the legion of good angels, to hurl Lucifer and the evil angels into a pit where the human creatures were under the sway of ideology and sexuality.

Because of his opposition to the divine will, Lucifer gradually came to be associated with Satan, from the Hebrew *Shai'tan* meaning "adversary", more commonly known as the Devil (accuser, slanderer).

In this way the supreme meaning was forgotten, that of the Heavenly rebel who lost his divine status and then wished to offer humanity the light required to show the way to spiritual illumination.

PANTEÓN DE HOMBRES ILUSTRES

Julián Gayarre, 3
• Metro: Menéndez Pelayo
• Open Monday–Friday from 9.30am to 6pm; Sundays and holidays from
9am to 3pm

This is one of the most beautiful, solitary and atypical places in Madrid. It contains a total of seven superb tombs (six inside, one outside) which are the work of such sculptors as Mariano Benlliure, Arturo Mélida y Alinari, Agustín Querol, Federico Aparici and Elías Martín. For some time, such famous figures as Diego Muñoz-Torrero, Eduardo Dato, Cánovas del Castillo, Práxedes Mateo Sagasta and Salustiano Olózaga were buried here; then, at various points, their mortal remains were reclaimed by their native cities. Today, the Pantheon houses the mortal remains of only one man: the politician José Canalejas (1854–1912).

An imposing pantheon for one man alone

Established by law in 1837, the Pantheon was first within the church of San Francisco el Grande, with the present building commissioned by Maria-Cristina of Austria in 1890. The designs were by the architect Fernando Arbós y Tremanti, who took his inspiration for this magnificent combination of Byzantine and Neo-Renaissance from Florence's bell tower (Campanile de Giotto), on which Giotto had begun work in 1334.

CITY OF THE LOST DEAD

Curiously, the mortal remains of a number of major figures in the history of Spain and of Madrid have been "mislaid". This is the case, for example, with the bodies of the writers Calderón de la Barca, Lope de Vega and Miguel de Cervantes. The author of *Don Quixote* died in 1616 and was buried in the monastery of Las Trinitarias Descalzas, (No. 18 Calle Lope de Vega). On the façade is a plaque commemorating the fact, but there is no physical trace of his tomb. As for Lope de Vega himself, he was buried in 1635 in the church of San Sebastian (No. 38 Calle Atocha), but all trace of the body was lost after the renovation of the parish cemetery. Finally, the body of Calderón de la Barca (1600–1681) was transferred from the Pantheon of Famous Men to the Church of Los Dolores (No. 103 Calle San Bernardo), where all trace of it was lost after the building was destroyed in 1936 during the Civil War. It is thought that his bones were placed in safe-keeping; but the curate who said he knew where they had been hidden died years ago without revealing his secret. Similarly, the mortal remains of Velázquez have never been identified, and the head of Goya is who knows where (see p. 73).

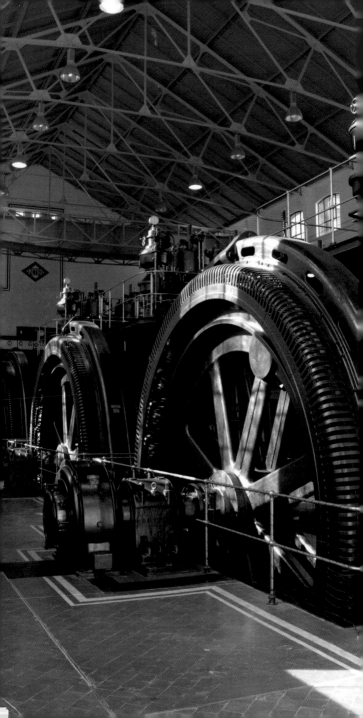

"MOTORES DE PACÍFICO" HANGAR

Calle Valderribas, 49
• Open Tuesday–Friday from 11am to 7pm; Saturday, Sunday and public holidays from 11am to 3pm
• Admission free
• Metro: Pacífico, Conde de Casal

> **Engines of the former metro**

Rather like finding yourself in a back-to-the-future scene from the film *Metropolis*, the Motores de Pacífico hangar is impressive with its giant diesel engines. This former power station is now given over to telling the story of Madrid's underground engineering.

The Motores hangar, built between 1922 and 1923, came into service in 1924 to secure the electricity supply to the new metro network, whose first line was inaugurated in 1919 by King Alfonso XIII. Engineers José María and Manuel Otamendi, who were commissioned to install the machinery, were also responsible for constructing the metro. The building, for its part, was designed by Antonio Palacios, who extended the use of *azulejos* to additional sections of the city's transport system as a corporate image. This eminent architect put his name to some of the most characteristic buildings of the capital, such as the Palacio de Comunicaciones, now Madrid City Hall, the Círculo de Bellas Artes and the former Banco Central, which now houses the Instituto Cervantes.

At the time, the plant converted the energy that it received to power the metro tracks, but it could also generate its own power with its three gigantic diesel engines imported from Germany, with a capacity of 1,500 horsepower.

The plant, indicative of the steady development and modernisation of the city, had the greatest capacity in Spain at the time and also played a part in historic events. As the metro network served as a depot and refuge during the Civil War, the Motores hangar supplied the city with electricity when the shortages were at their worst. But while the electricity companies succeeded in guaranteeing a regular supply for the city, the machinery grew obsolete and the plant stopped work in 1972, finally closing in 1987.

For its opening to the general public, the building has now recovered its original appearance both externally and internally. The machinery and other components have been cleaned and restored. Obsolete, but shining again, dynamos, alternators and batteries give visitors an idea of their past history and hence that of the city.

MONUMENT TO A ROCKING GRANNY

• Metro: Puente de Vallecas

Your rocker friends dedicate this monument to you

O ne of the most unusual monuments to be seen in Madrid (and one of the few where the central figure is from popular culture) must be the one dedicated to Ángeles Rodríguez Hidalgo (1900–1993), better known in the 1980s as "la abuela rockera" (the rocker grandmother).

The bronze bust of the rocker grandmother, by artist Carmen Jorba, was placed in Calle de Peña Gorbea in 1998, five years after her death and two years after the legendary concert given in Sala Canciller by musicians such as Rosendo, Miguel Ríos, Esturión, Asfalto, Sobredosis and Ñu. This concert was held to raise funds for the monument and thus to pay tribute to a great friend of Spanish heavy metal. The Madrid Rock boutique and artist Mario Scasso made up the balance to meet the budget.

Ángeles Rodríguez Hidalgo, that elderly lady who never took off her leather jacket, Argentine-born and Madrileña by adoption, was above all an AC/DC fan. Her interest in rock and heavy metal began when she was already getting on in years, and throughout the 1980s she never missed a concert or festival, so became a very popular character much respected by young people. Her charisma and style of dress turned her into an endearing figure of the Spanish night, and her music knowledge livened up her "Abuela Consulta" (Granny's Advice) column in *Heavy Rock* magazine, in which she answered questions on the music she loved.

Ángeles Rodríguez Hidalgo was at the height of her popularity when the band Panzer chose a photo of her for the cover of their *Toca madera* album, where she is shown making a dismissive gesture. Her rocker friends wanted to immortalise her in this pose, although the sculpture is puzzling because it seems to show a raised fist, a gesture that owes more to communism than to heavy metal. When the statue was installed, the grandmother's hand did indeed have the first and little fingers raised, but this gesture dear to heavy metal fans was misread by the local residents as an allusion to the devil. So it was decided to cut off her fingers.

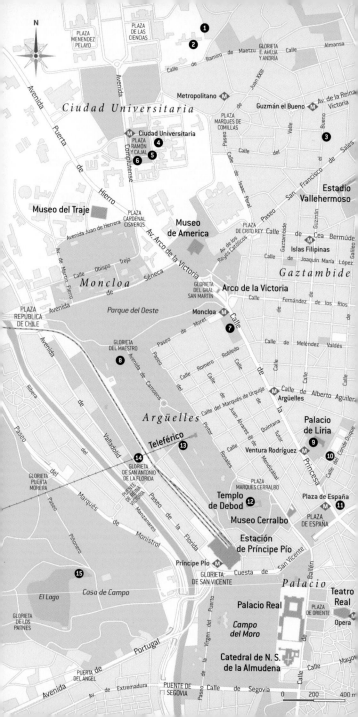

WEST

CAPIROTES OF LA DEHESA DE LA VILLA

La Dehesa de la Villa park
Francos Rodríguez, 79
• Metro: Francos Rodríguez

> *A subterranean water gallery*

Scattered about the parkland of La Dehesa de la Villa are eight peculiar stones in the shape of the tall pointed hoods worn by members of religious confraternities (*capirotes*). These are the visible traces of the former water channel (see p. xxx) that was part of a network of underground galleries supplying Madrid from the beginning of the seventeenth century until 1858, the year of the inauguration of the Isabella II canal.

Measuring about 70 centimetres high and 80 centimetres wide, the granite *capirotes* of La Dehesa de la Villa closed off the shafts giving access to the channel and also featured a ventilation shaft to the water below. They mark a section of the Amaniel water channel, also known as the "Viaje de Palacio" (Palace Route), built between 1614 and 1619 during the reign of Philip III, to supply the Alcazar. This channel began to the north of Madrid and then divided into two branches: one running through La Dehesa, and the other crossing the former Huerta del Obispo (bishop's kitchen garden). The two branches came together again before reaching Plaza de Oriented. Its total length was 6 kilometres.

These channels ended their course in the city's water fountains, where residents came to fill their jugs and pots, along with the water carriers who were employed to transport water from the fountains to the homes of those willing to pay for the service. The system was very well-organised but had a few drawbacks, and although new sections were built, the water supply was always insufficient. The city was divided into districts and each was endowed with a precise number of fountains, pipes, water carriers, and a given quantity of water. Over time, the system was perfected with the installation of "neighbourhood pipes", exclusively reserved to local residents as the name suggests. But "water thieves" also began to operate: they opened holes along the watercourse. These problems, along with the lack of hygiene at certain fountains where animals were allowed to drink, constituted a real headache for the administrators of the city's water supply, notably in view of the speed with which sickness and epidemics spread.

FISH FARM OF THE SCHOOL OF FORESTRY ENGINEERING   ❷

Technical University of Madrid
Calle de las Moreras, s/n
• Tel: 91 336 50 40
• Metro: Ciudad Universitaria

Trout breeding in the heart of Madrid

The surprisingly central fish farm of the School of Forestry Engineering is quite unique in its way. The site is reached through a large arboretum where over 4,000 species of plants are kept for research.

Although visitors are free to stroll around the area reserved for fish farming, it is best to book in advance to benefit from expert commentaries.

The pisciculture centre is organised into a system of terraces whereby water runs down through a network of channels into different basins, each carrying an explanation as to the species being bred there. The red and black spotted trout, native to the rivers around Madrid and currently under threat of extinction, is the star attraction.

The method followed by the school is to take samples from the wild which, after spawning, are put back into their rivers of origin. The indigenous trout are fragile and therefore difficult to breed in captivity, because they originate in mountain streams and so need high-quality water to simulate their natural environment. This is why researchers at the centre use oxygen-rich, low-temperature water taken from the Madrid aquifer, a 200 metre deep well.

As well as the outdoor basins, you can also visit the aquaria on the ground floor of the main building. These contain a diversity of species suited to pisciculture, along with information on their characteristics and habitats.

The facility is designed for research as well as a visitor attraction. Its aim is not intensive farming, although some of the fish reared there can be used in ecological projects. Some trout, for example, are kept for reproduction purposes, while others are introduced into controlled fishing environments with a strict no-kill policy, whereby landed fish are put straight back into the water.

MUSEUM OF THE *GUARDIA CIVIL*

Guzmán el Bueno, 110
• Metro: Guzmán el Bueno
• Open Monday—Friday from 9am to 1pm
• Admission free on presentation of ID

> **The moustache, a symbol of virility!**

Often overlooked, the museum of the Guardia Civil (Civil Guard) offers a very interesting collection of weapons and other memorabilia illustrating the history of this Spanish police force since it was set up in 1844.

On the second floor of one of the small buildings within the complex housing the national headquarters of the Guardia Civil, a variety of rifles, pistols, and other guns are on view, some of them true collectors' items, incrusted with precious stones. In the display rooms, you can learn not only about weapons and flags, but also the history of the tricorne hat (the traditional headgear of the Civil Guards) and different uniforms worn by policemen over the years. Curiously, a royal ordinance made it obligatory for policemen to sport moustaches to distinguish them from ordinary citizens. It even specified that their moustaches must be thick and bushy enough to emphasise their manliness! Many men of the period failed to make the grade for this reason, and others had to resort to subterfuge to present an acceptable moustache.

Another surprising item in the collection is a box that every policeman had to have on his person. It contained cleaning tools but also a 25 peseta note (equivalent to three months' salary) to ensure that the holder would never ask for a loan.

You can also see a regulation bicycle dating from 1865 with a Mauser rifle and the large cape worn while patrolling the city; various enormous, obsolete communication devices; and a large number of commemorative objects, as well as scale models explaining the history of the police.

PROFESSOR REVERTE COMA MUSEUM OF FORENSIC ANTHROPOLOGY

4

Faculty of Medicine, Complutense University of Madrid
• Tel: 91 394 15 78
• Access on request
• Metro: Ciudad Universitaria

Crime and punishment

The Museum of Forensic Anthropology offers a detailed insight into everything relating to the world of crime. Built up thanks to the determination of Professor Reverte Coma, the collection is divided into twenty sections which range from ancient skulls, giving a historical perspective into violent death, to items connected with more recent legal cases.

One of the most remarkable exhibits in this vast collection is perhaps the *garrote vil*, a garrotte that originally came from the prison of Carabanchel. The instrument was used for executions and consists of an iron collar which, when the screw was tightened by the executioner, would break the neck of the accused.

The *garrote vil* was one of the legal methods of execution in Spain between 1820 and 1978, when the new Constitution abolished the death penalty. The

last to be executed by garrotte were the anarchist Salvador Puig Antich and the mysterious German miscreant, Heinz Ches, on 2 March 1974, under the Franco regime.

The museum, originally set up as a research and experimental resource for medical and forensic students studying criminology, is now open to the public, but only by booking on certain days.

HISPANIC PHARMACY MUSEUM ❺

Faculty of Pharmacy, Complutense University of Madrid
Plaza de Ramón y Cajal, s/n
• Morning visits on request
• Tel: 91 394 17 97
• Metro: Ciudad Universitaria

> ***How were medicines made 200 years ago?***

The Hispanic Pharmacy Museum contains a vast range of material relative to the fabrication, conservation and administration of drugs down the centuries. The collections of colourful wooden boxes, ceramic jars and mortars and pestles are not to be missed, together with the exhibition of complete old-style dispensaries including an eighteenth-century Catalan drugstore, a fourteenth-century Hispano-Arab pharmacy complete with instruments typically used in alchemy, and an original reconstitution of the pharmacy from the San Juan Bautista de Astorga hospital.

OLD PHARMACIES IN MADRID

There are three long-established pharmacies in Madrid that give a good idea of the history of the city's drugstores. The first of these, the oldest, is **Real Botica de la Reina Madre** at 59 calle Major. Founded in 1578, the shop takes its name from the fact that the Queen Consort and Regent of Spain, Maria Christina, ordered her medicine here in the nineteenth century. The current pharmacy is in a 1913 building, typical of the Madrid modernist Art Nouveau style, and houses an interesting collection of mortars, weighing scales and other pharmaceutical equipment.

Farmacia Deleuze, at 39 calle San Bernado, is similarly full of charm, with its palatial feel and ornate Baroque decoration. As a municipal plaque at the entrance records, it was founded towards the end of the reign of Charles III of Spain in 1780. In 1990, the current owners undertook a meticulous room-by-room restoration and today customers are welcomed by the store's enormous chandelier, floral ceiling paintings and the Moorish and Rococo-style shelving. You can even have a quick look in the back room, which houses a fine collection of traditional jars from the Royal Porcelain Factory of Buen Retiro. The same area also served as a meeting place for politicians and intellectuals such as Espronceda and Ventura de la Vega before the city saw, in the course of the nineteenth century, the proliferation of cafés and the public discussions that made them so famous.

Farmacia Juanse, on the corner of San Andrés and San Vicente Ferrer streets, is both more recent (1892) and more popular. The strikingly colourful frescoes decorating the façade are an outstanding feature of this establishment. Made with traditional *azulejos*,* they advertise products

from the original Juanse laboratory that have long since disappeared, such as its "Pelletier" laxative tea, "El elefante" porous plasters for kidney pain or "Lombricina" anti-worm remedy. The appealing illustrations praising the virtues of these various potions are highly original.

Real Botica de la Reina Madre. Calle Mayor, 59. Metro: Sol or Opera
Farmacia Deleuze. San Bernardo, 39. Metro: Noviciado
Farmacia Juanse. Corner of San Andrés and San Vicente Ferrer. Metro: Tribunal

*azulejos: coloured ceramic tiling with a predominance of blue.

INSTITUTO DEL PATRIMONIO CULTURAL DE ESPAÑA ❻

Pintor El Greco, 4
• Metro: Ciudad Universitaria
• Tel: 91 550 44 00
• Open daily from 9.30am to 2pm
• Admission free on presentation of ID

"Crown of Thorns" building

The building that houses the Instituto de Patrimonio Cultural de España (Spanish Cultural Heritage Institute), better known as the "Crown of Thorns," is without a doubt one of the most striking examples of contemporary Spanish architecture. Designed in an organic, expressionist style, it is the work of architects Fernando Higueras and Antonio Miró. They were commissioned in 1965 by the Fine Arts directorate of the Ministry of Culture to create a restoration centre for works of art. Construction began in 1966 but was interrupted three years later when the Fine Arts director then in office proposed converting it into a National Centre for the Arts and Culture. The project had to be adapted to this purpose. Subsequently, it served as a Centre of Contemporary Art, as headquarters of the Spanish University by Correspondence, as the library of Madrid's Complutense University, and as the seat of the Spanish Constitutional Court. Finally, in 1985 it became home to the Instituto del Patrimonio Cultural de España.

The circular edifice with a radius of 40 metres is divided into thirty principal sections matching the sixty modules (two per section) forming the façade, which is crowned by a series of concrete spikes – hence the nickname. Two concentric rings facilitate circulation around each of the four floors linked by stairways and lifts. A third outer ring gives lorries access to the workshops originally conceived for restoring artworks of great size.

Inside, a glass roof reinforced by a metal structure supplys the building with ample light. After presenting your ID at the reception, you can admire the beauty of the installations, watch restoration work on historical paintings from the corridors, and enter the circular library, designed by the same architects, whose furnishings reproduce the spiked mouldings outside.

UFOS AT THE SPANISH AIR FORCE HEADQUARTERS LIBRARY

❼

Princesa, 2
• Metro: Moncloa
• Open Monday–Friday from 9am to 2pm

Military studies of UFOs

Entering a military building closely guarded by a throng of policemen and barriers is not impossible. Strange as it may seem, you only need to present your ID at reception and express an interest in UFOs.

In the library of the headquarters of the Spanish Air Force, visitors can consult seventy-five files, declassified between 1992 and 1999, concerning UFO observations in Spain: 2,000 pages relating 100 separate cases, most of them dating from the 1960s and 1970s.

Information that was once top secret is now available to anyone interested, although a majority of visitors are those claiming to have witnessed extraterrestrial phenomena. To reach the library, you need to pass through the long dreary corridors of this building inspired by El Escorial monastery and the Prado Museum, built at the behest of the dictator Franco between 1942 and 1951, on the former site of Modelo prison. The decor dates from the 1970s, and the chance of meeting other civilians is slim: you are now in the bowels of an active military headquarters dealing with matters of state.

Most of the files were drawn up by the Air Force staff and record in extreme detail the impressions of pilots having observed spacecraft "shaped like squid, with two lateral lights, and executing ascending movements". Much of the documentation explains that due to a strange phenomenon blurring films, it was impossible to obtain visible evidence. Other accounts tell of static metallic objects, bright noiseless vessels, multicoloured spearheads, and blinding lights. Among the reports, you can also read the transcripts of exchanges between airline pilots and the control tower, explaining that they are witnessing strange unidentified flying objects.

EXTRATERRESTRIALS IN SPAIN

The first written account of an incident resembling an UFO encounter can be found in the *Avisos históricos* (Historical Notices) dating from 1639. The chronicler José Pellicer de Ossau y Tovar mentions the passage of a "globe of fire or a light ... like that of the Sun on a hazy day, which gave off increasing heat".

It was only in the twentieth century that the Spanish military began to record such observations in secret reports. The strangest case recorded in Spain was that experienced by Fernando Sesma, founder in 1954 of the Sociedad de Amigos de los Visitantes del Espacio (Society of Friends of Visitors from Outer Space), whose motto is "believe everything unless proved otherwise". The members of this club meet in La Ballena Alegre (The Jolly Whale) in the cellar of the former Café Lyon. Sesma has fascinated UFO fans, journalists and other listeners with his tales of messages transmitted by Saliano, an extraterrestrial from the planet Auco. It was finally revealed that he wrote the messages himself, although he has never admitted this.

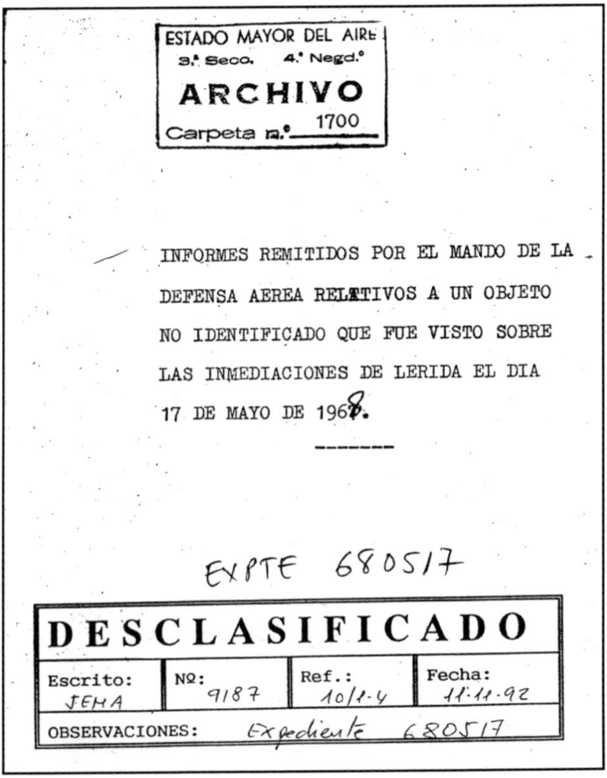

ESTADO MAYOR DEL AIRE
3.ª Secc.   4.ª Negd.º

ARCHIVO

Carpeta n.º _____ 1700

INFORMES REMITIDOS POR EL MANDO DE LA DEFENSA AEREA RELATIVOS A UN OBJETO NO IDENTIFICADO QUE FUE VISTO SOBRE LAS INMEDIACIONES DE LERIDA EL DIA 17 DE MAYO DE 1968.

————

EXPTE 680517

DESCLASIFICADO

Escrito: JEMA	Nº: 9187	Ref.: 10/1.4	Fecha: 11.11.92
OBSERVACIONES:	Expediente 680517		

LA TINAJA

Parque del Oeste
• Metro: Moncloa

*A giant
former
ceramics kiln*

I n the centre of Oeste Park you'll find, hidden among the shrubbery, an earthenware jar (*tinaja*) measuring over 15 metres in height, with a locked door. In fact a giant kiln, it belonged to the Real Fábrica de La Moncloa, a ceramics factory built in 1817 by order of Queen Maria Isabel of Braganza, the wife of King Ferdinand VII, to replace the Real Fábrica del Buen Retiro, another factory that was destroyed during the War of Independence against the French (see page 33).

The kiln, considered as an important example of industrial architecture, dates from after the construction of the factory itself. It is believed to have been built in 1881, and although it has deteriorated due to exposure to the weather and lack of maintenance, there is a project to transform it into an exhibition space for the nearby Escuela Madrileña de Cerámica La Moncloa (School of Ceramic Arts). This school is the last vestige of the former factory which was forced to close at the end of the nineteenth century, after the Zuloaga brothers took charge of its operations. Despite their great talent, the running costs of the factory and lack of public demand led to bankruptcy.

To reach La Tinaja, we suggest you enter the park from Calle Pintor Rosales, walk down Paseo Jacinto y Francisco Alcántara as far as the fountain, and then turn left. La Tinaja is in the grounds of a police station, and to get a good look at it you'll need to ask permission.

GUIDED TOURS OF PALACIO DE LIRIA

Calle Princesa, 20
• Tours by appointment only, between October and May
• Tel: 91 547 53 02
• Metro: Ventura Rodriguez

Family treasures

Calle Princesa is so called after the first daughter of Queen Isabella II. At No. 20 stands the Palacio de Liria, home to the Duchess of Alba and the largest private residence in the capital.

Part of the palace is open to the public, although the number of guided tours is limited. The waiting list is long and only a restricted number of people are admitted each week. Still, it is worth making the effort: this is an exceptional and little-known private art collection, one of the very few which has survived the centuries undiminished.

With paintings by Goya, Van Loo, Titian and Federico de Madrazo, the Portrait Gallery is the centrepiece of the visit. But there are also masterpieces by Fra Angelico, Rembrandt, Dürer, Veronese, Van Dyck, Rubens, El Greco, Zurbarán and Ribera – as well as the remarkable *The Duke of Liria receiving the Order of the Golden Fleece*, the only example of Ingres' work in Spain.

Over the years the duchess further enriched the collection by acquiring works by such nineteenth- and twentieth-century masters as Picasso, Miró, Chagall and Renoir. Finally, there is a library whose collection of historic documents is of inestimable value; for example, it includes letters written by Christopher Columbus.

Considered the "younger brother" of the Royal Palace, this *palacio* was built in three stages during the course of the eighteenth century, with three architects working on the project at different times: the Frenchman Guilbert, the Spaniard Rodriguez and the Italian Sabatini. Other architects have also worked on the various restoration and refurbishment schemes in the palace – most notably after the damage suffered during the Civil War. However, from the street there is no sign of the main façade or any suggestion of the precious treasures within. All you can see are the extraordinary statues that protect the gate and railings: female figures in a feline pose, whose bared claws and unnerving glare are intended to intimidate the curious and hold them at bay.

COMPOSICION

OFERTA ESPECIAL

SOFA 3 PLAZAS   975.-€
SOFA 2 PLAZAS   725.-€
3+2 PLAZAS   1.450.-€

FRESCOES OF THE RUSTIKA SHOP

San Bernardino, 3
• Tel: 91 541 94 17
• Metro: Plaza de España

> *Frescoes by Zuloaga in a former piano factory*

Nothing would let you guess that two art treasures can be found among the furniture and other decorative objects in the Rustika shop: frescoes by the painter and ceramicist Daniel Zuloaga (1852–1921), and a ticket booth from the former Montano concert hall, which once stood on this site.

The concert hall, along with a piano factory in a neighbouring building (No. 4 Calle Dos Amigos), belonged to the Montano family, who were great lovers of classical music and devoted themselves from 1838 to the manufacture of Spanish pianos. Although there is no trace of what became of the Montano pianos, they seem to have been highly prized in their time.

The building which today holds the furniture shop was constructed by another member of the Montano family, and a moulding with the initial "M" of the family name can still be seen on the façade. Along with the concert hall, it dates from the turn of the twentieth century, long after the factory was built.

The Rustika frescoes by Zuloaga are an additional pleasant surprise. He is particularly known for his contribution to the exterior decoration and architecture of several famous buildings in Madrid, including the Velázquez Palace in Buen Retiro park and the Ministry of Agriculture building. Here, in a totally unexpected place, we have another example of his artistic talent.

IMPRENTA ARTESANAL DEL AYUNTAMIENTO ⑪ DE MADRID

Conde Duque, 9
- Open Monday—Friday from 9am to 1.30pm
- Guided tours on request only: 91 588 57 68

Books before modern printing

The Imprenta Artesanal del Ayuntamiento de Madrid (Craft Printing House of Madrid's City Council) preserves traditional book printing and binding techniques. Visiting this workshop also gives you insight into the craft's traditional methods, from composing texts with movable type to hand-sewn rustic binding. These rare editions are made on manual machines, some of which date from the nineteenth century and others from the early twentieth century. Among the unique objects collected here is a Linotype, a machine that is part typewriter and part mini metal foundry. Using a keyboard, a full line of text is composed in a single block of lead, thus speeding up typesetting.

Also on show is the extraordinary collection of engraving plates and binder stamps of Antolín Palomino, the greatest Spanish authority on binding techniques.

The guided tour is a chance to admire the daily work of the bookbinders and printers: the patience with which they paste the covers and sew the pages, the way they gild and decorate books in the binding workshop, or the way the restorers combat the typical problems of antique books, such as humidity, mould and acidity. At the end of the tour, you can pause for a while to admire the magnificent collection of artistic bindings.

"OLVIDOTECA": A LIBRARY OF FORGOTTEN BOOKS

Conde Duque Hotel - Plaza Conde Valle Suchil, 5
- Tel. 91 447 70 00 • Metro: San Bernardo

Conde Duque Hotel has had the great idea of setting up a new type of library: all the books that visitors have left behind. Although at first the collection only consisted of a few books in a glass case, with time it has grown and has ultimately come to fill a large space. The list of books available is quite long. The majority of them are paperbacks in English, but you'll also find books in a dozen or so other languages: guidebooks, self-help books, art books, books on natural medicine, best-sellers, or classics of literature. A rather nice feature of this library is that since it was started many guests have deliberately left books behind to add to the original collection.

ESOTERIC SYMBOLISM OF THE TEMPLE OF DEBOD

Templo de Debod
Parque del Oeste

12

> *From Egypt to the Freemasons*

Carefully dismantled and then reassembled in Spain, the Temple of Debod was officially opened on 20 July 1972 and is the largest Egyptian temple to be found anywhere outside Egypt. It was during work on the Aswan Dam that a "Spanish Committee", headed by the professor and archaeologist Martin Almagro Basch, was set up to protect the Nubian temples that would be flooded as a result of the project. It was this committee that oversaw the dismantling and transfer of the Temple of Debod, which had stood on Elephantine island in the Nile. The Egyptian Government presented this monument to Spain in 1968. However, the blocks of stone remained on Elephantine until April 1970, when they were shipped to Alexandria. On 6 June that same year, they were crated up and loaded on the *Benisa*, arriving in the port of Valencia on 18 June. From there they were taken by lorry to Madrid, being first stored in the building of the Cuartel de la Montaña and then moved to Parque del Oeste.

The iconography of the Temple of Debod is clearly concordant with the Western tradition of esoteric spiritualism. Thus the Spanish Freemasons immediately saw significance in the paintings of the "Chain of Union", in which gods and pharaohs hold each other by the hand: the image reflects a ritual that is a traditional part of Freemasonry and is an expression of fraternity and mutual aid.

As in the Grand Lodge of Spain, the symbolism of twinned columns is associated with power and equilibrium.

Similarly, the Eye of Horus (*ujat* or *wedjat*) amulet in the temple sanctuary can be related to the Eye of the Divine Providence of the Great Architect of the Universe, while the three structures of the building correspond to the three levels of Masonic initiation: the degrees of Entered Apprentice, Fellow Craft and Master Mason.

Freemasonry claims that its historical origins are to be found in Egypt before the Flood, its foundation dating from 1370 BC, when – esoteric tradition has it – the pharaoh Akhenaton (Amenhotep IV) together with his queen Nefertiti established the cult of the Sun god Amon-Ra within the Great Pyramid of Cheops.

In Madrid, the Temple of Debod has been set within an artificial lake, so its present site reflects its original location: all Egyptian temples included a sacred lake, whose waters were normally drawn from groundwater basins fed by the Nile. Such lakes represented the primordial waters that had existed before the creation of the world.

VALOR
HEROISMO
N PUEBLO

JE QUE LE TRIBUTAN
TOS CON ORGULLO
FIQUEN A ESPAÑA.

OR A SUS
HEROES,

). AYUNTAMIENTO
DRID
UNICIPAL DE MONCLOA
MAYO 1982

MEMORIAL TO THE MASSACRES OF 3 MAY 1808

Cemetery of La Florida
Parque del Oeste
Calle de Francisco y Jacinto Alcantara, 4
• Visits only on Saturday and Sunday mornings in May and June; or by request at 91 588 16 36 (town hall)
• asturt@telefonica.net
• Metro: Principe Pio

> *Goya's heroes are buried here*

The cemetery of La Florida may be the least well-known of Madrid's cemeteries, but it is a real gem in the heart of the capital. Nestling in the calm greenery of the Parque del Oeste, the small enclosure dating from 1796 bears the traces of one of the most symbolic events in the town's long history: it holds the remains of the forty-three Madrilene rebels executed by French soldiers under General Murat at the foot of the Montaña del Príncipe Pío on the morning of 3 May 1808.

In fact, over 200 citizens were shot on that fateful day, following a popular uprising against the occupation of the city by Napoleon's troops.

The destiny of those who now rest in the cemetery was sealed when they were drawn by lot from among the many rebels rounded up during the insurrection of 2 May. They were tortured, shot and thrown into a common grave; but a few days later, the brothers from the Buena Dicha congregation retrieved the bodies and secretly buried them in the small cemetery belonging to the Hermitage of San Antonio de la Florida and normally reserved for employees of the royal palace.

These tragic events were immortalised with extraordinary poignancy by Goya in his painting *Los fusilamientos del 3 de mayo* (*Execution of the Defenders of Madrid, 3rd May, 1808*), which is reproduced in *azulejos* at the entrance to the cemetery.

Until recently, only nineteen of the bodies had been identified, but the names of ten others have come to light over the last few years. A commemorative plaque records their names, while the other unidentified victims rest in their anonymity.

Since 1917, the Sociedad Filantrópica de Milicianos (Philanthropic Militiamen's Society) has been responsible for the upkeep of the site, which for many years was closed to visitors. After restoration, it was opened to the public on 2 May 1981 but closed again due to vandalism. Following the bicentenary celebrations of 2 May 2008, it was decided that visits would be allowed only on Saturday and Sunday mornings in May and June. Nevertheless, it is still possible (and well worthwhile) to visit the cemetery at other times by special permission, obtainable from the town hall or the Sociedad Filantrópica de Milicianos.

STRANGE STORY OF GOYA'S SKULL

The body of the Spanish artist Francisco de Goya lies buried in the small, superb Hermitage of San Antonio de la Florida. But only his body, because his head has never been found.

There have been numerous theories concerning the fate of Goya's skull. Among them two, equally strange, are considered to be the most plausible.

The first involves the Asturian painter Dionisio Fierros (1827–1894): according to Goya's biographer, Antonina Vallentin, in the mid nineteenth century a canvas painted by Fierros bore the following inscription: "Goya's skull painted by Fierros in 1849". Vallentin's research led her to Fierros's widow and grandson, who claimed that there was a skull in the painter's studio and it could have belonged to Goya. Unfortunately, the painting disappeared without leaving a trace. However, according to the book by Vicente Muñoz Puelles, *El cráneo de Goya* ("Goya's Skull"), the skull remained in Fierros's studio until one of his nephews, a student in medicine, decided to perform some experiments on the expansive force of gases by soaking some chickpeas in the alleged skull of Goya. The skull broke, and the nephew, not knowing what to do with the remnants, gave them to a dog to gnaw on.

The main character in the other theory is Doctor Laffargue, a friend of the artist, who was authorised by Goya to cut off his head upon his death in order to pursue his studies in phrenology (the analysis of the character of an individual according to the shape of their skull), a field which was very much in vogue at the time. The skull may have been sent from Bordeaux to Paris, but was then lost.

There is a more romantic version: Goya asked the executors of his will to sever his head after his death and bury it in Madrid, next to the right foot of the Duchess of Alba, who was the great love of his life.

But none of these theories could have been formulated without Joaquín Pereyra, the Spanish consul in Bordeaux from 1880. It was there that Pereyra discovered the tomb of Francisco de Goya y Lucientes in Chartreuse cemetery and who was amazed to discover, on exhumation, a body without a head.

Goya's headless corpse had to wait nearly nineteen years before it was reburied. Pereyra did everything in his power, but the administrative services concerned were unwilling to pay for repatriation or a funeral service worthy of this artistic genius.

ORGANIC URBAN HORTICULTURE COURSES   🄮

Richard Schirrmann youth hostel
Casa de Campo
• Free courses
• www.asociaciongrama.org
• Metro: Lago or Batàn

> ## *School for horticulturists*

Since 2004, this small horticultural school has been teaching soil preparation and growing techniques that ban the use of chemical fertilisers and pesticides, as well as giving practical tips on everything from weeding to building your own drip-watering system. Once students are familiar with natural fertilisation methods and with the use of basic gardening tools, they can move on to sowing seeds. The third phase of the course is more technical, consisting essentially of practical advice on crop rotation to prevent blight while avoiding soil impoverishment.

These courses in ecological urban gardening are completely free and include both theory and practical work where students learn about the horticultural profession.

The project is an initiative from the Grupo de Acciòn para el Medio Ambiente (GRAMA), an environmental action group dedicated to the protection of the ecosystem. As well as urban allotments, GRAMA is involved in issues of urban waste management, reclaiming natural sites degraded by man and promoting awareness among the Spanish public of the diversity of the country's natural spaces. GRAMA's activities, which also include organised walks in the Madrid area, are detailed on its website.

BECOME AN ACROBAT OR A JUGGLER

The Carampa circus school is just a stone's throw from the horticultural centre. This meeting-place for circus lovers provides a two-year professional training programme, but also runs specialised classes in acrobatics, clowning, gymnastics, balance and tightrope walking, pantomime and dance. There are also regular shows featuring top-class performers in a traditional if somewhat modest circus atmosphere. For further information, call 91 479 26 02.

WHITE STORK RESCUE CENTRE

Casa de Campo Information Centre
Near Paseo del Embarcadero del Lago
• Tel: 91 479 60 02
• Metro: Lago or Principe Pio

> *A "clinic"
> for storks
> in Casa
> de Campo*

Tucked away right in the heart of Madrid's biggest park, Casa de Campo, the Centro de Recuperacion de la Cigüena Blanca (White Stork Rescue Centre) comes as quite a surprise: a nature sanctuary, in the middle of the capital city, giving visitors the chance to learn about storks and their way of life.

This "clinic" is set up to allow storks to nest and reproduce there, providing the necessary care resources in a natural habitat protected from the pollution of city life. Some of the birds arrive with slight injuries and are treated and fed until they can fend for themselves, while others will never be able to survive independently and are looked after accordingly.

The storks are put into quarantine as soon as they arrive, in order to build up their natural defences weakened by the stress of town life. They can then wander freely around the centre, which has its own pond.

The park also has a butterfly centre. Note that visits are only possible by booking far enough in advance and must respect the quarterly activity programme drawn up by the municipal environmental service.

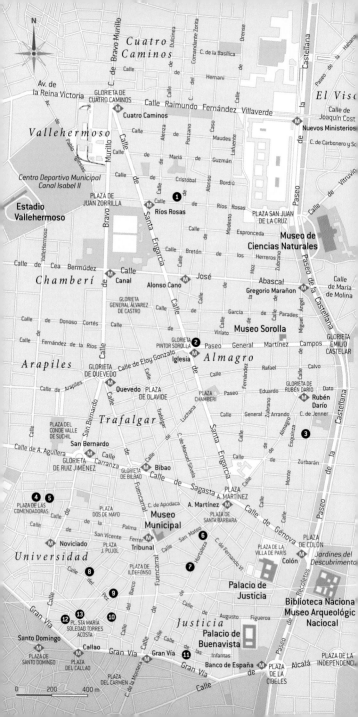

NORTH

UNDERGROUND MINE OF THE MINING SCHOOL

Calle Ríos Rosas, 21
• Guided tours of the mine on request: 91 336 70 23
• Admission free

Underground mine in the centre of Madrid!

In the courtyard of the Academy of Mining Engineers in calle Ríos Rosas, near Paseo de la Castellana, you'll find the entrance to a really unique mine from which no ore has ever been extracted as it was just used for student experiments.

The Marcelo Jorissen experimental mine is named after the man who was director of the school in 1967, and who commissioned the work that year. Since then, the mine has been converted into a simple and original museum where visitors are introduced to some traditional mining techniques.

The mine consists of a vertical well 15 metres deep with a wrought iron armature through which the cages of men and equipment descended, as well as a gallery that goes as far as calle Ríos Rosas.

You enter through a large opening before climbing down a ladder with seventy-five rungs, gradually descending into the humid depths of the mine. At the bottom, a gallery opens out before you with mining cars parked on the rail tracks running through it. The tour lets you examine different types of timbering (used to shore up the galleries), beams and coffering. All these details give an insight into the various excavation methods used at the time the mine was constructed. For example, you learn that eucalyptus was preferred to any other type of beam because the wood creaked under stress, giving the miners time to reach safety in case the roof caved in.

The most beguiling aspect of this site is the authenticity of features such as the armature, mining cars, rail tracks and stones that support the underground line, which come from actual mining operations. Although the vein of coal at the bottom of the mine is, of course, fake (it's made from coloured earth), the ambience lets you imagine working conditions here in the depths of the earth with great realism.

MUSEO HISTÓRICO MINERO DON FELIPE DE BORBÓN Y GRECIA
The building of the Academy of Mining Engineers, an artistic and historic monument, also houses the Don Felipe de Borbón y Grecia Historic Mining Museum, whose varied collection illustrates the rich mining traditions of Spain and Europe since the eighteenth century. Admission free.

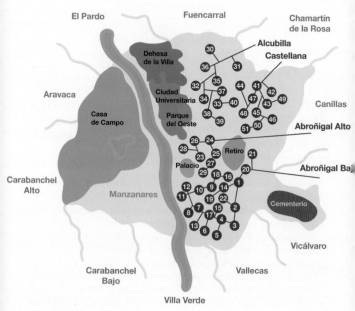

Viajes de Agua - Madrid 1847

Abroñigal Bajo
1. Cibeles
2. San Juan
3. Santa Isabel
4. Ave María
5. Lavapiés
6. Cabestreros
7. Cerrillo del Rastro
8. Toledo
9. Puerta Cerrada
10. Puerta Moros
11. Águila
12. Rosario
13. Embajadores
14. Alcalá. *Caño de vecindad*
15. Plaza de Jesús. *Caño de vecindad*
16. El Sordo. *Caño de vecindad*
17. Plaza del Rastro. *Caño de vecindad*
18. C. de la Paloma. *Caño de vecindad*
19. C. de la Segovia. *Caño de vecindad*
20. San Bruno. *Caño de vecindad*
21. San Blas. *Caño de vecindad*
22. Apolo. *Caño de vecindad*

Abroñigal Alto
23. Celenque
24. Aduana
25. Relatores
26. Plaza de La Villa
27. Cebada
28. C. de los Magros.
Caño de vecindad
29. Lavapiés.
Caño de vecindad

Castellana
30. San Fernando
31. San Antón
32. Valverde
33. Red de San Luis
34. Santo Domingo
35. Mostenses
36. Afligidos
37. Chamberí.
Caño de vecindad
38. Plaza del Gato.
Caño de vecindad
39. Tudescos.
Caño de vecindad
40. Hospicio.
Caño de vecindad

Alcubilla
41. Galápagos
42. Del Soldado
43. Plaza de Bilbao
44. Descalzas
45. Santa Ana
46. Antón Martín
47. Santa Cruz
48. Preciados.
Caño de vecindad
49. Regueros.
Caño de vecindad
50. San Gregorio.
Caño de vecindad
51. De los Gitanos.
Caño de vecindad

MANHOLE COVER OF CALLE SANTA ENGRACIA ❷

Santa Engracia, 73
• Metro: Iglesia

Former water route

On the pavement just in front of No. 73 Calle Santa Engracia, you'll find a manhole cover that is quite different from all the others in the city. On it are inscribed the words "Viaje antiguo del agua" (Former Water Route).

In the past, the water distribution network was entirely different from that existing today. Before the inauguration of the Canal de Isabel II (now the public company that manages Madrid's water supply), in the mid nineteenth century, water was tapped at various spots around Madrid. There was also a network of underground galleries and wells inherited from the Arabs that became obsolete as the city grew (at the time, Madrid had 200,000 inhabitants).

The main sites supplying drinking water (Abroñigal Alto, Abroñigal Bajo, Alcubilla and Castellana) belonged to the city of Madrid and were thus public, although there were also private sources such as Fuente del Berro, a crown property.

Over time these underground canals fell into disuse and many of them were destroyed in the construction of car parks and tunnels. However, a few lengths of the network remain unused or serve to hold different types of cables. They aren't currently open to visitors, but hopefully in the near future

a curious public will be able to explore the bowels of Madrid.

The sewer of Calle Santa Engracia is a reminder of the "Viaje de la Alcubilla" (Alcubilla Route), a passage that specialised technicians used to access the old network.

The Viaje de la Alcubilla dates from 1399 and originates in the Dehesa de Chamartín, which lies 18 metres deep in the Alcubilla Valley. The line followed the road to Calle Bravo Murillo and what is now Glorieta de Cuatro Caminos before branching a little farther along into two: Calle Santa Engracia and towards Glorieta de Quevedo.

To see other vestiges of the old water network, you can visit La Dehesa de la Villa park (p. 47).

VESTIGES OF THE BETI-JAI COURT ❸

Marqués de Riscal, 7
• Metro: Rubén Darío

> **Last pelota court in Madrid**

Behind the façade of the dilapidated building at No. 7 calle Marqués de Riscal, you'll find the remains of the Beti-Jai court, the last "industrial" pelota court in the world (designed in the nineteenth century and no longer erected next to the large walls of churches or in village squares). The Beti-Jai court is also the last pelota court in Madrid and the only example of nineteenth-century sporting facility architecture in the city.

The Beti-Jai court was extravagant: Andalusian-style ceramic plinths, Neo-Mudejar details, stands that could hold up to 4,000 people, and a court 67 metres long where all the different forms of Basque pelota could be played. In Spain, this sport was more popular than football, at least in the nineteenth and early twentieth centuries.

Construction of the Beti-Jai court, whose name is Basque for "party all the time", began in 1893 at the bequest of businessman José Arana, who wanted to create a court in the image of the Beti-Jai of San Sebastian, but bigger and in the most modern materials of the time.

The site, designed by architect Joaquín Rucoba who was also responsible for the Arriaga theatre and the town hall of Bilbao, was inaugurated on 29 April 1894. It included lounges, a main hall, ticket booths, a cafeteria, an infirmary, rooms for the athletes and administrative offices. It soon became a meeting place for Madrid's middle class.

The court closed its doors in 1919. The site was converted into a police station, a garage, and even into a rehearsal hall for a Falangist band. Nowadays, the court (4,000 square metres in one of the most elegant districts of Madrid) is waiting its turn to be restored.

SACRISTÍA DE LOS CABALLEROS

Las Comendadoras de Santiago convent
Calle del Acuerdo, 19 ·
• Metro: Noviciado
• Tours: first Monday of the month at 4pm, phone to book a place
• Tel: 91 548 1842

> **Where the Knights of the Order of St James were appointed**

The magnificent Sacristía de los Caballeros (Sacristy of the Knights) in Las Comendadoras de Santiago convent (built between 1584 and 1697), is a fascinating site that is indiscernible from the street.

Here men would prepare themselves before being appointed a knight of the Order of St James. The ceremony itself took place in the adjacent church. This large Baroque salon was painted in the three colours of the sisters of the convent: green to represent laurels; yellow for the conquered lands; and red for the blood spilt by the martyrs.

It took months of restoration to rediscover these three original colours. The walls had been covered entirely in white and grey, firstly because of the stubbornness of an architect who believed that all colours were the work of the devil, but mainly because of the plague. Indeed, one of the layers removed carried the following inscription: "I, a painter from Cordoba, in 1914, whitewashed the walls to disinfect them from the plague."

The sacristy of the knights, the work of Francisco de Moradillo, was built between 1746 and 1753, during the reign of Ferdinand VI. The murals evoke some of the secrets of the time. For example, it is said that the roses in the vases are Louis XVI roses and that they came to decorate the sacristy in the same year that they were cultivated for the very first time.

In one corner of the sacristy you'll also find the beautiful Fuente de los Tritones (Fountain of the Tritons), where the future knights bathed before being called by the bell that invited them to move to the next room. There, the nuns passed the knights a light meal through a hatch so as not to be seen. The bell and hatch have also been restored.

LA CAPILLA DE LAS NIÑAS

Calle del Acuerdo, 19
• Metro: Noviciado
• Tours: first Monday of the month at 4pm; phone to book a place
• Tel: 91 548 1842

> ## Another little-known jewel

The guided tour of the Sacristía de los Caballeros (see preceding double page) includes a visit to the very charming Capilla de las Niñas (Chapel of the Young Girls), which has also recovered its past splendour thanks to painstaking restoration work. The chapel, decorated in red and pink tones, owes its name to the period when knights left to protect pilgrims following the Way of St James or to repel the Muslims, leaving their wives and daughters in the care of the nuns.

On the chapel ceiling is the first Bourbon coat of arms known in Madrid. Its design is strange, as it is entirely back to front: the images that were supposed to be on the right were put on the left, and vice versa – the result of a painter's error.

On the right wall of the chapel, you can also see the portrait of a nun of the Order of the Commandresses of Santiago dressed in the religious habit of her Order and bearing the cross of St James on her chest, which is rarely found on the robes of cloistered nuns. This portrait depicts the founder of the Order, whose mortal remains also rest in the chapel. Curiously, her bones were found in Valladolid and brought to Madrid after a series of complications and, around the same time, the painting was bought in Germany, not knowing that the nun depicted in the portrait was the Order's founder. The coffin was placed near the small altar, and on it you'll find a magnificent hand-woven mantle and a date symbolising the journey taken by the remains before finding their final resting-place: "Mariana Vélez Ladrón de Guevara (1681–2009)". The chapel also possesses a painting by Luca Giordano dating from 1695 that has recently been restored. With masterful strokes, Giordano portrays St James during the Battle of Clavijo, which took place on 23 May 844 and is considered legendary because of the saint's miraculous intervention.

LIZARD HOUSE

Mejía Lequerica, 1
• Metro: Alonso Martínez

In the jungle of Madrid

Casa de los Lagartos (Lizard House) owes its name to the giant lizards holding up its cornice. This building that Benito González designed to hold rented flats is also unique in the fact that its façade is eleven times longer than it is wide. So from San Mateo and Hortaleza streets, you can see that the building is just 5 metres wide.

The town's Sanitation Committee, which believed that more space was needed for interior courtyards, threatened to kill off the project, but the architect resolved the problem by placing the staircase in the middle of the building and making only two flats on each floor. All the rooms of the flats, even the bathroom, were open to the exterior. A metal structure allowed for the addition of many windows to let in the light.

This building is also unique in that it is one of Madrid's rare examples of the Vienna Secession movement, the main characteristic of which is geometric simplicity and the symmetry of decorative elements.

Thanks to its recent restoration, the building has recovered the magnificent decor that adheres to the guiding principles of the Vienna School led by Otto Wagner. However, the original white colour has been replaced by an ochre shade that offers better resistance to pollution.

BLESSING OF ANIMALS

Hortaleza, 72
- Metro: Alonso Martínez o Chueca
- Day of blessing: 17 January

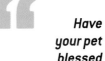

Have your pet blessed

Every year on 17 January, San Antón church welcomes hundreds of pets for a celebration in honour of St Anthony, the patron saint of animals. Legend says that this saint of Egyptian origin, who was always accompanied by a pig, cared for all the injured animals he came across.

On the day of the celebration, you'll see parrots, cats, dogs, fish, turtles and even boas patiently waiting to be blessed by the priest with the following words: "Lord, bless this animal and may Saint Anthony protect them from all harm." Then, the owners receive a piece of bread that was prepared in such a way so that it doesn't go stale. According to tradition, this bread is not eaten but is instead kept in a cupboard near a coin so as not to invalidate the blessing. Afterwards, the owners and their pets walk in procession through the neighbourhood, accompanied by a few zoo animals, the mounted police, army carrier pigeons and fire dogs.

Banned from 1619 to 1725, this celebration was brought back into favour during the reign of Ferdinand VII. It was suspended again twice, but it has been celebrated regularly since 1985.

ST ANTHONY AND THE ANIMALS

St Anthony was born in Egypt in the third century and it is believed that he lived to be over 100 years old. At a young age, he sold everything he owned and lived an ascetic life dedicated to prayer. He became a hermit and set out on a long voyage through the desert, during which he was often prey to temptation, but he never gave in. Because of his lifestyle and devotion, many people followed in his footsteps. His special relationship with animals is explained in a legend that tells of the day when a wild sow came up to him with her blind offspring. The saint healed them and, to show her gratitude, the sow refused to leave his side, protecting him from danger. Later, many animals joined them. The Christians considered this to be a supreme gift because if St Anthony dominated the animals, then he was also dominating creation ...

SCULPTURE OF A FISH

Calle del Pez at the corner of calle de Jesús del Valle
Metro: Noviciado

> *The legend of calle del Pez*

The little fish carved on the building at the corner of calle del Pez and calle de Jesús del Valle is at the origin of this street name that dates back to the seventeenth century. At the time, the section between Pozas and San Bernardo streets was called calle de la Fuente del Cura (Priest's Fountain). Indeed, Diego Henríquez, a priest of noble lineage, lived on a beautiful estate at this spot. Henríquez's property included five ponds, a fountain and a small pool filled with fish of all colours which he showed to neighbours and churchgoers every year on 24 June, the feast day of St John.

When the priest died, Philip II, who had already moved his court to Madrid, acquired the estate and divided it up to build housing. Juan Coronel bought the section of the estate with the pool and fish, which became the pets of his daughter, Blanca. Unfortunately, after all the restoration and bricklaying work, the fish started dying off one by one. Blanca saved the last survivor and placed it in an aquarium, but despite her painstaking care the little fish didn't survive. To console his daughter, Juan Coronel had a fish carved in stone by the door of the house and, next to it, he hung a sign reading "Casa del Pez" (House of the Fish). Years later, Blanca took the veil at the neighbouring San Plácido convent. The convent quickly fell into disgrace: twenty-six of the thirty nuns who lived there were possessed by the devil. Over time, the Coronel house was destroyed, but the fish was kept and placed on a new building.

CHRIST OF VELÁZQUEZ: REMINDER OF A KING'S LOVE FOR A NUN

San Plácido convent (see above) was also the theatre for another scandal. Indeed, King Philip IV fell in love with a nun and had a passage built from the house next door to the convent so he could access her chambers. The night of the tryst, the prioress saw to it that the pretty Sister Margarita dressed all in black and appeared to be as rigid as a corpse; she even placed a crucifix at her bedside. Believing her dead, Philip IV gave the convent a clock that tolled the hours in a tone fit for a funeral. In memory of this incident, the king instructed Velázquez to paint the Christ that is now housed in the Prado and known as the *Christ of Velázquez*.

VAULT OF SAN ANTONIO DE LOS ALEMANES CHURCH ❾

Corredera Baja de San Pablo, 16
• Open Monday–Friday, from 11am to 12pm and 7pm to 8pm; Saturday and Sunday, 11.30am to 1.30pm
• Metro: Gran Vía

A dazzling and little-known vault

The church of San Antonio de los Alemanes (St Anthony of the Germans) is one-of-a-kind in Madrid. Hidden behind austere walls directly in the city centre, it is far from the tourist track. When you enter, you'll be surprised by this ellipsoidal space entirely covered (walls and vault) in frescoes depicting scenes from the life of St Anthony of Padua (1195–1231), the patron saint of travellers, the poor, bricklayers, paper-makers and barren women. The scenes are very theatrical, as was customary at the time since prominent dramatists and authors (Lope de Vega, Tirso de Molina and Calderón de la Barca) kept very close ties with religion. Influenced by this very popular theatrical spirit, churches also looked to create places that would project a religious feeling to motivate the congregation.

The central theme of the vault, entitled *The Celestial Apotheosis of Saint Anthony*, is the work of Francisco Carreño de Miranda and depicts the Portuguese saint ascending towards the Virgin who awaits him on a cloud, surrounded by angels. The paintings of the first altarpiece are by Vicente Carducho, a contemporary of Velázquez, and the magnificent main altarpiece is by Miguel Fernández. The sculptures are the work of Francisco Gutiérrez.

The church was founded in 1606 by Philip II who wanted to provide a place of worship for the Portuguese residents of Madrid. It was thus known as San Antonio of the Portuguese. When Portugal became independent, Mariana of Austria handed the church over to the German Catholics who arrived in Madrid with Maria Anna of Neuburg, the future wife of Charles II. Since 1702, the church has belonged to the Hermandad del Refugio (Brotherhood of the Refuge).

"ROUND OF BREAD AND EGG"

The Hermandad del Refugio was known for its charity work, known as the *"round of bread and egg"*. The purpose was to offer a hard-boiled egg, a piece of bread and shelter for the night to the homeless. As it happens the church has preserved a wooden gauge with a hole that was used to measure the eggs bought for the poor. Those that were too small were rejected because they didn't live up to the prestigious standards of the brotherhood.

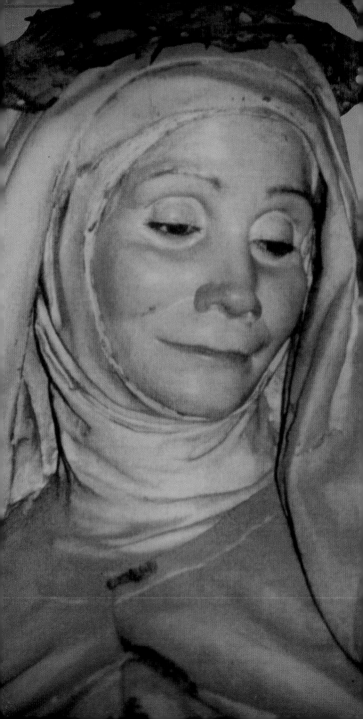

THE INCORRUPT BODY OF BLESSED MARIANA DE JESÚS

Colegio y Monasterio de las Madras Mercedarias de Don Juan de Alarcón
At the corner of Valverde, 15 and Puebla, 1
• Open Wednesday from 10am to 1pm; Mass Sunday and 17 April
• The incorrupt body of Blessed Mariana de Jesús is on view 17 April

> *Corpse that smells like apples*

To enter the church of the Convent of the Mercedarian Sisters of Don Juan de Alarcón, you have to ring the bell at the school gate and cross a courtyard that is often full of children. Nevertheless, a solemn silence fills the air on approaching the church: you are entering a sacred place where a future saint rests in peace.

You enter near the altar and once inside, you'll be attracted by the beauty and radiance of the large painting by Juan de Toledo (1611–1665), a Spanish painter and soldier who is better known for his paintings of war than for his religious works. The large painting that crowns the altar depicts the apotheosis of the Immaculate Virgin, who appears surrounded by angels.

The principle religious interest of this church is the fact that it is home to the incorrupt body of Blessed Mariana de Jesús, which is put on view every year on 17 April. The rest of the year, the coffin where she rests (a gift from Isabella II) remains closed. According to the nuns and the faithful, an aroma of apples wafts from the body of the Blessed sister.

This convent, which was originally named Nuestra Señora de la Concepción, was founded in 1609 by Priest Don Juan Pacheco de Alarcón. Little is known about its origin and construction, except that the church was completed in 1655 and later altered in 1671 by architect Gaspar de la Peña.

THE WOMAN WHO DISFIGURED HERSELF TO AVOID MARRIAGE

Mariana's life was marked by faith, self-flagellation, sacrifice, and her family's opposition to her decision to take the veil. It is said that she had many suitors, including Lope de Vega. Although she became engaged to a young man of high society, Mariana refused to marry and went so far as to disfigure herself, by cutting the corners of her mouth, to convince her father that God was the only man in her life.

Mariana entered the convent of the Mercedarians in 1606. She had many hallucinations (she affirmed many times that she had spoken to the Virgin and played with Baby Jesus), visions and moments of ecstasy. She died on 17 April 1624 and many people came to kiss her hands and feet. A fervent believer even went so far as to try to take one of her fingers. Three years later, her remains were exhumed, and to the great surprise of the doctors of Casa Real they discovered the body intact. The limbs were still flexible and the body gave off the aroma of apples.

ART GALLERY OF VÁZQUEZ DE MELLA CAR PARK

Plaza Vázquez de Mella
• Metro: Chueca

Vázquez de Mella public car park is rather unique: lines from *The Divine Comedy* are spread across its walls in red neon lights.

Rather a unique car park ...

Chueca An-Dante is the name chosen by the creator of this project, the Italian architect Teresa Sapey, who took her inspiration for the renovation of this car park from Dante Alighieri's Fifth Canto. In this canto, Dante enters the second circle of Hell, where he finds Minos who judges the lascivious. One of the phrases of this magnificent canto figures prominently on the walls of the car park: "*Amor, que amar oblige al que es amado, meató a sus brazos, con placer tan fuerte que, como ves, ni aun muerto me abandona*" ("Love, that exempts no one beloved from loving, seized me with pleasure of this man so strongly, that, as thou seest, it doth not yet desert me").

In fact, the car park serves as a gigantic art gallery: photographs of men, women and children in poses expressing love decorate its walls. The slick design is complemented with state-of-the-art technology, such as an optical registration plate reader and lights indicating how many parking spaces are available. At the entrance, or more precisely the entrance ramp, you'll find a sculpture of a large red ribbon – the city's tribute to the fight against AIDS.

DINING IN A CAR PARK ...

Strange as it may seem, the Chinese restaurant in the Plaza de España is indeed located in a car park. No one knows the real name of this tiny establishment, as the sign is only written in Chinese, and is simply known as the "Chinese place in the car park". But it has seven tables and a bar, and serves good food at reasonable prices. One other good feature is that, being underground, it's completely isolated and cell phones won't ring. So you can at last have lunch or dinner in peace.

LA BUENA DICHA CHURCH

Calle Silva, 25
- Metro: Callao
- Masses daily at 12 noon and 7pm

A most peculiar church

In a narrow street, wedged between tall buildings, you may come across the strange "good luck church", an architectural gem that escapes the attention of most passers-by in Madrid.

This church was built in 1916–1917 by Francisco García Nava, on a commission from the Marquis of Hinojales, in a highly eclectic style. The façade presents a mix of Gothic and Moorish elements, but the use of brick and the structure, composed of different volumes and curves, gives the building an undeniably modernist (Art Nouveau) character.

The history of this church really dates back to 1594, the year in which the friar Sebastián Villoslada founded on this same site La Buena Dicha hospital and created a brotherhood of sixteen priests and sixty-two lay members to administer it. Under the auspices of Our Lady of the Immaculate Conception or of Good Fortune, the brotherhood devoted itself to assisting the poor in the San Martín parish to which it belonged. The main entrance of this brotherhood was on Calle Libreros and the rear was occupied by a small cemetery, known as the Cementerio de la Buena Dicha (cemetery of good luck).

This brotherhood provided invaluable medical services during the insurrection of 2 May 1808 against Napoleon's troops occupying the city, and the great heroines of this period, such as Clara del Rey and Manuela Malasaña, were buried in the cemetery. At the end of the nineteenth century, the hospital and cemetery were demolished to make way for the existing church of La Buena Dicha, administered by the Brothers of Mercy.

DUEL IN CALLE DESENGAÑO

Just a short walk from La Buena Dicha church, the "street of disillusion" is one of the oldest in Madrid. It derives its name from a legend that two gentlemen, in love with the same woman, once decided to fight a duel here to win her favours. However a mysterious black shadow interrupted their combat. The duellists followed it, and the shadow turned around and removed its hood to reveal a decomposing face. The two horrified men exclaimed, "What disillusion!" because they saw this as a manifestation of the transitory nature of physical appearance.

COFFIN OF ALEXIA GONZÁLEZ BARROS

San Martín de Tours Church
Desengaño, 26
• Open daily from 6pm to 8.30pm
• Metro: Gran Vía

**A child
saint**

Although she has not yet been canonised by the Vatican, Alexia González Barros is considered by many Catholics to be a child saint. In fact, there is an association, "For the Beatification of Alexia", which receives the expressions of thanks of people who believe Alexia intervened positively in their lives through miraculous acts.

Known as "the servant of God", Alexia was a perfect little girl fascinated by religion and dedicated, like the rest of her family, to the Opus Dei. At the age of 13, she discovered she had a malignant tumour, which led to complications from which she never recovered. Some eight books, translated into several languages, have been written about her, and there is even a film based on her life (*Camino* by Spanish director Javier Fesser).

Her remains lie in San Martín de Tours church (right in the city centre) in a small, golden coffin that was a gift from the congregation.

The church, the construction of which began in 1725, has a simple brick façade flanked by a tower at each end. On the high altar is a painting by Ricardo Bellver depicting St Martin astride a horse.

CENTRE-EAST

STRONGROOM OF THE CERVANTES INSTITUTE ❶

Calle Alacalá, 49
• Tel: 91 436 76 00
• Visits in groups only: rei3@cervantes.es
• Metro: Banco de España

> *Where great artists store mementos of the future*

The basement of the Cervantes Institute contains a spectacular strongroom, designed by the architect Manuel Cabanyes in 1944 to house the safes and strongboxes of the bank that used to occupy this building. This little-known place now serves as the *Caja de las Letras* (Literary Strongroom).

Entry to the strongroom is by a massive circular door about 50 cm thick – state-of-the-art security technology at the time it was built. Laid out over two floors are some 1,800 strongboxes, as well as six small rooms for use by those who wished to examine the contents of their own box. However, in 2007 the purpose of this strongroom changed entirely: it has now become a custodian of memories, intended to resist the passage of time. Since that date the great figures of Spanish culture have used the strongboxes to store a secret legacy, which cannot be opened before the date established by the individual writer, artist, scientist, musician or architect invited to participate in the scheme.

Spanish writer Francisco Ayala was the first to place material in a strongbox: various books and a letter, which cannot be removed until 2057. Other Spanish-speaking artists represented there include Juan Gelman, Luis García Berlanga, José Emilio Pacheco, Ana Maria Matute and Antoni Tàpies.*

The Cervantes Institute, founded in 1991 to promote teaching of the Spanish language and international appreciation of Spanish culture, occupies the former premises of the Banco del Rio de la Plata, which subsequently became the Banco Central Hispano. The building was constructed in 1918 to designs by Antonio Palacios and Joaquin Otamendi, then extended in 1947. Later it was converted to house one of Spain's most prestigious cultural institutions. Certain parts of the old bank have remained intact: for example, the old cashier windows house the Institute's internet service. These windows are in the main hall and are part of the space used for exhibitions.

The Institute's hall also has a display of large-scale photographs of the old strongroom and the present-day *Caja de las Letras*.

---

*Gelman: Argentine poet; Berlanga: Spanish film director; Pacheco: Mexican essayist and poet; Matute: Spanish novelist; Tàpies: Catalan painter.

AN EXPLANATION FOR THE GHOSTS OF MADRID?

The House of the Seven Chimneys and San José church are not very far from Plaza de Cibeles, a truly enchanted place as well as the building which housed the Hospital del Corte and Buen Suceso church. Lucifer is said to have hidden a French officer in the clock tower of Buen Suceso, during the final defeat of Napoleon's troops, to save him from the wrath of the Spanish mob (see p. 127). The church was the only one to celebrate services late at night, which may partly explain the frequency of ghostly sightings. San José parish and Plaza de Cibeles are places where three water channels run underground. The electromagnetic and telluric energy may be more intense there and affect human senses to provoke paranormal or supernatural phenomena.

Nevertheless, some people find another possible explanation for these phenomena in the celebration of Adoración Nocturna (Nocturnal Worship). This tradition, founded by the brotherhoods of the Holy Sacrament, was started in Madrid by seven distinguished Catholics who on the night of 3 November 1877 celebrated a first night of worship in the church of the Capuchin monastery of El Prado, now gone but which once stood facing the existing building of the Congreso de los Diputados (lower house of Parliament). The institution of Adoración Nocturna made its appearance shortly after the abolition of the Inquisition (5 July 1834) and the spread of intellectual, artistic, and religious freedoms, leaving the field wide open to the ghosts of the past. Urban legends concerning spirits from the afterlife may have stemmed from the general astonishment at these religious services held at hours when bodies take their rest and souls roam freely.

LEGEND OF THE HOUSE OF THE SEVEN CHIMNEYS

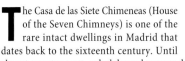

Plaza del Rey, 1
• Metro: Banco de España

A ghost on the roof

The Casa de las Siete Chimeneas (House of the Seven Chimneys) is one of the rare intact dwellings in Madrid that dates back to the sixteenth century. Until almost a century ago, a dark legend surrounded this building, which today houses the Spanish Ministry of Culture.

It is said that an illegitimate daughter of King Philip II once lived here. She married a captain who was killed fighting the French at the battle of St Quentin (1557). She died a few months later, from grief or perhaps murdered, the circumstances of her death never having been made clear. Some say that the widow was walled up in one of the rooms of the house, and later occupants apparently heard her footsteps. Neighbours even claimed to have seen a woman wearing gauzy white garments in the room, with a torch in her hand.

The House of the Seven Chimneys, commissioned by Pedro de Ledesma, was built between 1574 and 1577 by the architect Antonio Sillero. In 1583, the Genoese merchant Baltasar Cattaneo bought it and carried out the first modifications, including the roof with four gables and the strange seven chimneys. The house then became the property of Francisco Sansi y Mesa and the Colmenares family until 1716, and then passed to the counts of Polentinos.

Due to its character as a residence for the nobility (the Marquis of Esquilache also occupied it at one point) the building was the object of various renovations. During the last century, it became the headquarters for several banks. Neither the work carried out nor the succession of owners, however, has managed to dissipate the legend of the ghost walking among the seven chimneys.

SIGHTS NE.

SCULPTURES OF HALF-MEN, HALF-FISH
Calle del Barquillo, 8

The façade of the house at No. 8 Calle del Barquillo is decorated with monsters, half-men, half-fish, who seem to support the balconies on their shoulders. The building is the work of José Urioste y Velada, who was commissioned in 1904 to construct a palace for Adolfo Rúspoli y Godoy, Duke of Sueca and Alcudia. Six years later, Urioste (also responsible for the widening of the Gran Vía) completed this edifice with a square floor plan, containing two independent residences overlooking a rectangular central courtyard.

GHOSTS OF SAN JOSÉ CHURCH

Calle de Alcalá, 43
• Metro: Sevilla

> *St Joseph and the ghosts of Madrid*

The church of San José (St Joseph), at No. 43 Calle de Alcalà, is probably the favourite spot of the ghost hunters who seem to abound in the city.

The first ghost story associated with the church took place in the nineteenth century shortly after the expulsion in 1836 of the Discalced (barefooted) Carmelite monks of St Hermenegild who lived in the monastery to which San José church once belonged. They left behind only empty buildings and the ghosts of former residents. But a strange thing happened, one New Year's Eve. After dining with his family, a young man made his way to the ball that was being held in a palace owned by one of the capital's noble families. He had been observing the guests for some time when, at three o'clock in the morning, he saw the most beautiful girl he had ever laid eyes on enter the ballroom. He hastened to greet her and the pair danced for the rest of the night. It was almost morning when the girl said she had to go home. The couple walked hand-in-hand through the streets until they arrived at the San José church. "I stay here," the girl said. The young man thought she must be mistaken, but when she insisted he thought she was making fun of him, so left in a huff. The following day at noon, the young man again passed in front of the church and saw that a funeral was in progress. Driven by curiosity, he entered the church and approached the coffin to find out who had died. To his great fright, he saw lying there the girl with whom he had danced all night. Feeling faint, he left in a hurry but heard someone following him out of the church. It was another girl who wanted to know what had happened to him. When the young man told her his story, she said, "That girl was my cousin. She had always been in love with you, but she was too shy to approach you and speak to you. Yesterday, at three in the morning, she passed away …"

There is another version of this Madrid legend, although the names of the main characters are different: the boy was called John and was English, she was Elena de Mendoza and belonged to a noble family. The pair met at a costume ball during Carnival, on 12 October 1853.

This tale is the starting-point of many other stories that take place in and around the San José church involving supernatural sightings, such as the story of the House of the Seven Chimneys (see p. 111).

CASA RIERA'S ENIGMATIC GARDEN

⑤

Calle Marqués de Casa Riera, 1
• Metro: Sevilla

*The dark
legend
of Casa Riera*

The garden of Casa Riera is tucked away behind the gate that leads to the building at No. 1 Calle Marqués de Casa Riera. In theory it is open only to people working in the offices in that building; however, in the courtyard there is a cafeteria with a terrace open to the public – providing an opportunity to see this garden, which is associated with a tragic tale.

It is said that an ancestor of the Marquis of Casa Riera once found two bodies in his garden: a man who had been stabbed with a sword and a woman dressed in white. The murderers would never be discovered. All that is known is that the marquis's relative had a cypress tree planted at the spot where the crime was committed. Then, he abandoned the building, ordering that it should be left uninhabited for the life of the cypress tree. In a way his wish was respected, for none of the subsequent owners right up to the time of the building's demolition spent much time there.

The original Marquis of Casa Riera had obtained his title in 1834 for services to the Crown, and it was around the same time that he bought this mansion for his bride, Doña Mercedes Mora y Narváez. However, the couple spent little time here, living most of their later years in Paris. At the end of the nineteenth century the whole area was transformed, with many of the neighbouring religious foundations being expropriated. The monastery next door was demolished, as was this private residence – together with the garden and the cypress tree that had kept the owners of the building at bay. One descendant of the marquis, Alejandro Mora y Riera, then built a property on the site; but even he didn't spend much time here – perhaps again out of respect for the cypress legend.

In the early 1930s another building was erected here, to designs by the architect Rodriguez Avial. Right up to 1977 this was one of the main headquarters of the Francoist movement. For many years there was no garden at all. Then, in the 1990s, the landscape architects Carmen Añon and Myriam Silber created, on the same site as the garden associated with the mysterious legend, a green space that managed to be more in keeping with the style of the new building while preserving something of the atmosphere of the city in which the couple had been mysteriously murdered and the cypress tree planted.

The garden is surrounded by a path that runs beneath a bower of flowers and climbing plants. Altogether the place is as romantic as it is unnerving.

LIBRARY OF THE CHAMBER OF DEPUTIES ⑥

Carrera de San Jerónimo, 39
• Tel: 91 390 60 00 • www.congreso.es
• Metro: Sevilla
• For access, apply for a researcher's pass: download the form online and return it with two photos and a photocopy of your passport/identity card. Guided tours (maximum 55 people) on Saturday between 10.30am and 12.30pm
• "Open Days" once a year, on the anniversary of the Spanish Constitution (6 December)

> ## Madrid's most important nineteenth-century library

The library of the Chamber of Deputies is a truly magical place. An architectural composition that succeeds in combining quality of design with an intimate atmosphere, this is undoubtedly Madrid's most important nineteenth-century library.

Unfortunately, it is not included in the guided tour of the Congress building that takes place every Saturday, as the reading room is part of the library. So the only way to see it is to apply for a researcher's pass, which can easily be obtained (see above).

The reading room, designed by Arturo Mélida in 1885, is an oval space that rises over four floors and is lined with superb bookcases in cedar wood and mahogany. The ceiling is decorated with an allegory of *The Temple of the Law* by José Maria de Gamoneda.

The library collection focuses on the political history of contemporary Spain, but there are also rare fifteenth-century codicils and a large quantity of nineteenth-century publications, as well as manuscripts and eight incunabula.

The guided tour is fascinating and lets you see the other rooms in the Congress building – including the elliptical main vestibule, which is dominated by a statue of Queen Isabella II. Around this sculpture are the portraits of nineteen leading politicians of the nineteenth or twentieth centuries. Note also the mahogany table, which almost certainly is the very one on which the 1812 Constitution was signed.

MARKS LEFT BY GUNSHOTS FIRED DURING THE ATTEMPTED COUP OF 1981

When you are in the Chamber itself, look up and you'll see two bullet holes in the ceiling. These are evidence of one of the most difficult moments in contemporary Spanish history: the attempted *coup d'état* of 23 February 1981.

ATTEND A CONGRESS SESSION

The Chamber of Deputies in Madrid allows each adult citizen the chance to watch the Congress at work. All you have to do is turn up with an identity card on Friday between 6pm and 2am; the entrance is the one in Calle Zorrilla.

CANNONS TURNED INTO LIONS

The lions that stand guard over the entrance to the Congress are by Ponciano Ponzano. They were made using the bronze from enemy cannons seized during the African War of 1859–60.

serie del Madrid Palace -
Director-Gerente: OTTO KERCHER
Madrid,

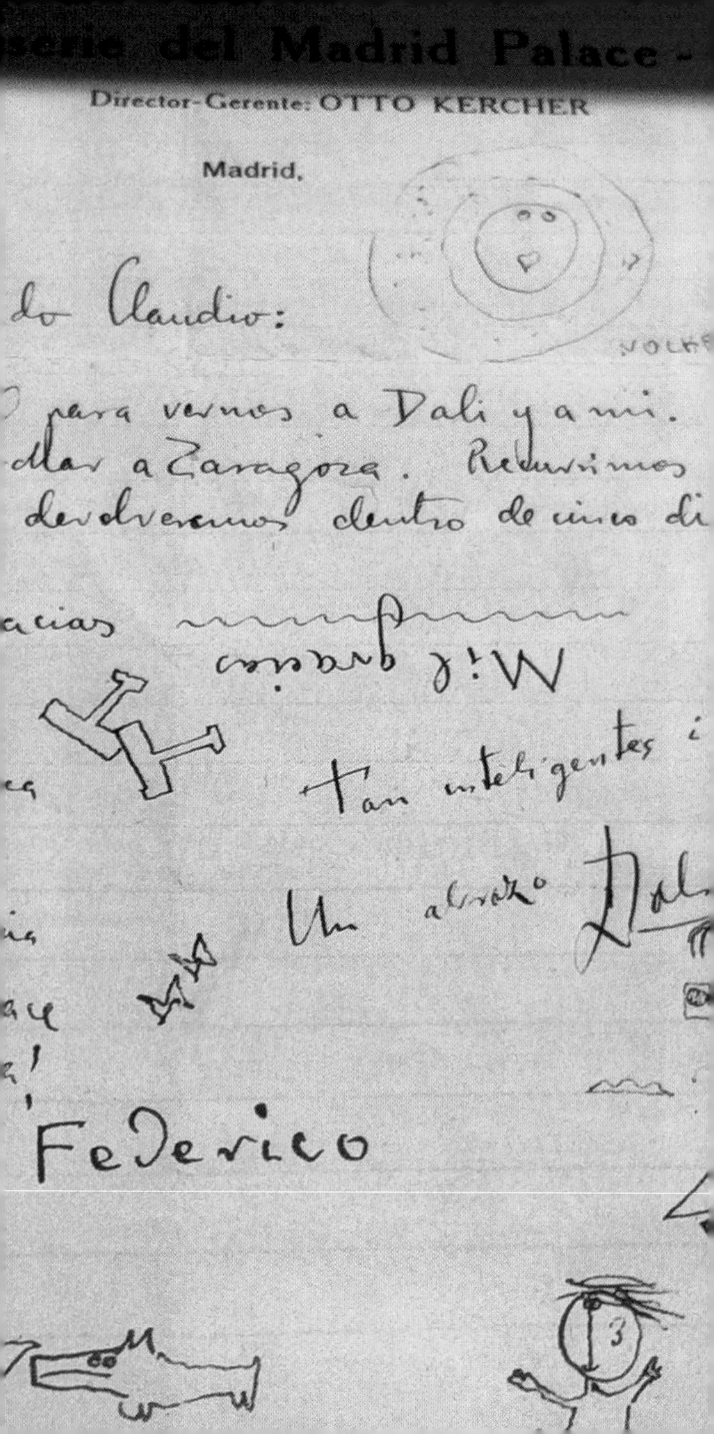

do Claudio:

para vernos a Dali y a mi.
llar a Zaragoza. Recibiremos
devolveremos dentro de cinco di

acias

Mil gracias

ca
Tan inteligentes i

ia
Un abrazo Dalí

ace

a!

Federico

COLLECTION OF THE "PALACE SPACE"

Westin Palace Hotel
Plaza de las Cortes, 7
• Tel: 91 360 8000
• Metro: Sevilla

> **When Lorca and Dali demanded money for Buñuel!**

Off one corner of the lobby of the legendary Westin Palace Hotel there is a small room known as the "Palace Space" which houses a collection of objects including a very remarkable letter. It bears the heading of the magnificent Brasserie of the Madrid Palace Hotel and is addressed to Claudio de la Torre, a novelist, poet, playwright and film director from the Canary Islands. In the letter, Salvador Dalí and Federico García Lorca demand 125 pesetas so that Luis Buñuel, who had "spent all his money," could make a trip to Saragossa. Alongside drawings by Dalí, there are a few verses by Lorca explaining how Buñuel was an assiduous patron of the hotel bar!

Next to this letter by Dalí and Lorca, you can see a *presse à canard* ("duck crusher", a special instrument used in making culinary sauces) that featured in the hotel's restaurant, as well as several photos of the hotel's inauguration by King Alfonso XIII. There are also the first room keys, hotel registers, greeting cards, silver coffee pots, oil lamps, candlesticks, and other memorabilia evoking past eras and visits by illustrious guests: Marlon Brando, the Dalai Lama, Buster Keaton, Hemingway, and Mata Hari herself.

SURGICAL OPERATIONS IN A BALLROOM DURING THE SPANISH CIVIL WAR!

During the Civil War, the hotel was converted into a hospital and the ballroom (now La Rotonda restaurant) was the place designated to carry out surgical operations, due to the light from its stained-glass dome.
Many years later, in more peaceful times, Argentine author Jorge Luis Borges made this room one of his favourite spots, precisely because the dome allowed him to catch a glimpse of the Sun's rays despite his near-blindness.

PEDRO ALMODÓVAR'S MADRID

Madrid is an essential part of the setting of all Pedro Almodóvar's films. Certain areas of the city which the director has used to create the atmosphere in his films have since become representative of his work.

On the seventh floor at No. 7 Calle Montalbán is the apartment where Carmen Maura lives in *Mujeres al borde de un ataque de nervios (Women on the Verge of a Nervous Breakdown)*.

At No. 15 in Plaza Santa Ana is a bar with a kitsch Arab-Andalusian decor. Called Villa Rosa, this curious place has lost its charm with the passage of time, and it is here that, in a scene in *Tacones lejanos (High Heels)*, Miguel Bosé in femme-fatale drag sings Luz Casala's *Un año de amor*.

At No. 38 Calle Almagro is the home of Antonio Banderas' family in *Mujeres al borde de un ataque de nervios*, while at No. 3 Calle Sevilla is the house occupied by the eponymous heroine of *Kika*.

Another building characteristic of the city which Almodóvar has used is No. 6 Calle Bordadores: in the film *¡Átame! (Tie Me Up; Tie Me Down)*. This is the home of the porn actress Marina, played by Victoria Abril.

The Maria Guerrero Theatre (No. 4 Calle Tamayo y Baus) is currently home to the Centro Dramático Nacional (National Drama Centre) and was the third theatre to be built in Madrid, following the Comedia and the Price. Designed by the architect Agustín Ortiz del Villajos, it was built in 1884 at the behest of the Marquis of Monasterio, and it was here that the character Becky del Páramo, played by Marisa Paredes, makes her stage comeback in *¡Átame!*. The character's apartment is in Plaza del Alamillo, in La Latina district.

Built in 1919 to designs by Antonio Palacios, the Círculo de Bellas Artes (Fine Arts Club) is located at No. 42 Calle de Alcalá and is characteristic of Madrid architecture. In the cafeteria here Peter Coyote and Victoria Abril discuss formats for reality shows in *Kika*.

At No. 18 Paseo de Eduardo Dato is the house occupied by Javier Bardem and Francesca Neri (David and Helena) in the film *Carne trémula (Live Flesh)*. The end sequence of that film was shot in Calle Arenal, done up for the occasion as if it were Christmas.

Almodóvar has also used the city's famous monuments: Plaza Mayor features in *La flor de mi secreto (The Flower of My Secret)* and Puerta de Alcalá appears at the beginning of *Carne trémula*. Other locations include Barajas airport, the AVE station at Atocha and Almudena cemetery.

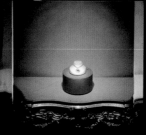

MUSEO

PRIVATE MUSEUM AT GRASSY THE JEWELLER'S

⑧

Gran Vía, 1
- Tel: 91 532 1007
- By appointment
- Open Monday–Friday from 10am to 2pm and 5pm to 8pm
- Metro: Gran Vía or Banco de España

Alejandro Grassy's personal collection

A telephone call will get you an appointment to visit the small and little-known museum of old clocks and watches in the basement of Grassy the Jeweller's. Opened in 1953, this discreet museum contains the private collection of Alejandro Grassy, the shop's founder. There are all kinds of timepieces: desk clocks, pendulum clocks, stand clocks, pocket watches and Empire-style clocks. Though most of the pieces are French, English or German, the museum also has a superb collection of eighteenth-century Japanese clocks. All currently working – or in working order – the clocks not only tell the time but have a clear decorative function, revealing how (from the fifteenth century

onwards) the timepiece had become the statement of a certain lifestyle.

Please note that, due to lack of space, large groups are not admitted. There is also limited information with regard to the pieces on display: just a few facts about date, place of origin and type.

The jewellery store itself is in an eclectic building designed in 1916 by Eladio Laredo.

NEARBY

HOTEL WITH A VIEW

⑨

On the fifth floor of the Petit Palace Alcalá Hotel (No. 2 Virgen de los Peligros) is the El Bilbaíno restaurant, which affords magnificent views of the Calle de Alcalá and the various characteristic buildings that line it. From here you can see: the cupolas of the Alcázar Theatre (No. 20 Alcalá), the chariots atop the Banco de Bilbao, and the old Equitativa Building (corner of No. 14 Alcalá and No. 3 Sevilla); the latter has numerous ornamental details, including sculptured elephant heads supporting the balcony on the first floor.

CASINO MILITAR – CULTURAL CENTRE OF THE ARMED FORCES

⑩

GHQ of Spanish Armed Forces
Gran Vía, 13
• Tel: 91 522 24 09
• Metro: Gran Vía

*Madrid
a century ago*

While the Casino Militar which houses the Armed Forces Cultural Centre is reserved to forces personnel and registered members, there is a public restaurant on the second floor – a chance to explore at least part of the building.

The Casino Militar, built in 1916–1919 to designs by Eduardo Sanchez Eznarriagat, was intended as a sports and leisure facility for members of the armed forces, to replace the facility in Plaza Santa Ana demolished to make way for the building of the Reina Victoria Hotel.

Whereas the original intention may have been to provide services exclusively for members, over time a number of facilities have been opened to the public. These include the gym, the fencing hall and the restaurant that offers a magnificent view along the Gran Via.

In the gym itself, located in the basement, time seems to have stood still: one piece of equipment is an early twentieth-century exercise cycle, which still works perfectly. As for the wonderful fencing hall, it is the oldest in Europe; covering a total area of 100 square metres, it also contains a collection of old foils and rapiers.

Two floors are given over to a hotel which, at reduced rates, provides rooms for servicemen and their families. There is also a hairdresser and a library, where heating is provided by a metal pipe that runs by the readers' feet. This room also has a collection of miniatures illustrating the uniforms of the Spanish Navy over the ages.

The vast entrance hall leads into a spacious marble ballroom, with a magnificent Art Nouveau glass ceiling.

In short, this is a place that has kept its early twentieth-century looks, when building work was just beginning on the Gran Via and Madrid was gradually being transformed into a great metropolis.

SYMBOLIC TRADITION IN PUERTA DEL SOL: STORIES OF LUCIFER AND VENUS

The name "Sun Gateway" came from the depiction of the Sun which graced the entrance to a fifteenth-century fortress that once stood here. Facing east, that fortification and its Sun emblem disappeared over time, but its symbolic function was taken over in the nineteenth century by the clock of the Casa de Correos, the oldest surviving building in the city. Traditionally, *madrileños* gather beneath this clock to greet the New Year. What few people know is that the twelve strokes of midnight on that occasion are linked to a story about Lucifer.

This famous clock (not, however, the present-day clock) was formerly part of the church of Buen Suceso, which at the time was abandoned and was finally dismantled. The story associated with it states that on 2 November 1812, when Madrid was occupied by Napoleonic forces, a captain of the French dragoons, together with some of his soldiers, took refuge in the clock tower, fleeing from a rebellion by the local population. When the *madrileños* discovered their hiding-place, they surrounded the Casa de Correos. The soldiers managed to escape, but the fate of the captain is unknown.

Legend has it that Lucifer hid him inside the clock. This story came about because in their meticulous search the rebels went through everywhere, including the clock mechanism, where they found nothing but a small mouse. Hence, to explain the man's disappearance, it was said that the devil had turned him into a mouse to help him escape.

So it is claimed that the twelve strokes of the clock at Puerta Del Sol that mark the advent of the New Year serve to ward off Lucifer. Remember, however, that very name Lucifer means "light bearer" (*lux fero*, see page 35) and was also the Roman name for the planet Venus, the first star visible at the dawn of the new year. Thus, the first day of the year is lit by Lucifer – or Venus – the "morning star" which is the central figure in this patriotic urban legend.

Due to the similarity of their daily trajectories across the sky, Venus has also been associated with the Sun. Ancient peoples such as the Celts and the Romans considered Venus to be a divine star, the messenger that intercedes between the divinity of the Sun and humankind. This is perhaps why an image of the Sun stood at Puerta del Sol, the geographical heart of Madrid and the starting-point of all the various roads out of the city.

CURIOUS ORIGIN AND DEVELOPMENT OF THE NAME "MADRID"

Built on the left bank of the Manzanares, Madrid was elevated to the rank of capital by Philip II in June 1541, when he transferred his court of 30,000 people here from Toledo. The arrival of the court triggered rapid development, with the building of the residences, churches and monasteries that would become the centre of urban life within the city.

According to the chroniclers of the day, the decision to make Madrid the new seat of political power within the ancient kingdom of *Hispania* was made because, at the time, this was a sort of paradisiacal oasis of gardens and woodlands, of fertile plains and bubbling fountains – all set against a background of unfailingly blue sky.

The fertility of the place meant that hunting and agriculture could produce enough to feed the limited population of the day. Furthermore, to shield the place against the unpleasant effects of the strong winds of the Sierra de Guadarrama, huge trees were planted, adding to the location's calm and freshness.

The oldest references to Madrid in chronicles date back to the tenth century, with the site where Philip V built his royal palace described as a "fortress".

Etymologically, the name "Madrid" can be traced back to the Celtic languages which subsequently became part of the languages of the other peoples who settled in the lands along the Manzanares. Archaeological evidence now confirms that there was human settlement in this region as early as the Palaeolithic, with communities of people in the Neolithic, Bronze and Iron Ages.

The Celts used the term *magos* to refer to a "plain", its range of reference ultimately expanding to embrace the concept of "market". *Magos* accounts for the first part of the name Madrid, the second coming from the Celtic term *ritum*, used to refer to areas through which rivers flowed. The Celtic *Magoritum* was then corrupted during the time of Arab rule into *Magerit* (pronounced *Madjerit*), thence becoming *Madrit* and finally Madrid.

The name *Magoritum* passed from the Celts to the Romans, who would also give the city the name *Osoria* – later *Ursaria* – because of the sizeable population of bears (in Latin: *ursa*) in the region, and because the local peoples defended themselves like bears against invaders.

Having no knowledge of the civilisations subsequently rediscovered by scholarly research, certain writers in the seventeenth to nineteenth centuries aimed to model the birth of Madrid on that of other great European cities and develop their own mythological account of its origins. Some, for example, incorrectly claimed that Madrid had been called *Metragirta* or *Mantua Carpetana*, and that it had been founded by Ocnus Bianor, son of Tiber, King of Tuscany, and of the beautiful Mantua.

At the end of the ninth century, the Arabs under the rule of Caliph Mohammed I (son of Abderraman II and the fifth independent Emir of Cordoba) built a fortress on a hill on the right bank of the Manzanares. It was thus that Madrid took on the form of a veritable city within a society that was more pastoral than urban.

The variations of the Arab name *Magerit* included *Madjerit*, *Mageridum*, *Magritum*, *Matritum*, *Mayrit*, etc. The famous inhabitants of that Muslim Madrid included the astronomer and mathematician Abul-Qasim Maslama. After the reconquest of Toledo by Alfonso VI of Castile, Madrid came under Christian rule but would then pass back under Arab control.

The alternation between the two did not end until the final consolidation of Christian rule in 1085, when Mayrit the Muslim became Madrid the Roman.

A pre-Muslim origin for the name is the term *Mayrit*, which refers to the river flowing between two hills opposite the city; the place was also known as *Matriz*, "Mother of Two Waters". Indeed, the term *Mayrit* is composed of the Arabic word *mayra* (mother) and the Iberian-Roman suffix *it*, meaning "place".

In which case, Madrid is the "Mother of Two Waters", an allusion to the Garden of Eden which was the site of the Creation; thus "Madrid" could also be an allusion to the "Mother of God".

COAT OF ARMS OF CASA CORDERO

Corner of Calles Esparteros and Mayor
• Metro: Sol

> *Lottery that allowed the construction of an emblematic building*

At the corner of Calles Esparteros and Mayor, the coat of arms held up by two stone bears is often taken to be the emblem of the property developer Santiago Alonso Cordero, which actually consisted of two lambs and a golden castle. It is more likely to be linked with Cordero's native village, Santiago Millas, in the province of León.

The wheel in the centre may be a reference to the lifestyle of the *maragatos* (a nickname given to the local residents): they were great travellers who roamed throughout western and central Spain in their wagons, selling craft goods. Casa Cordero is also known as Casa del Maragato. Alonso Cordero, a man so remarkable that he features in certain pages of *Episodios nacionales* ("National Episodes") by the great Spanish novelist Benito Pérez Galdós, was often seen wearing the typical costume of the *maragato*.

The construction of this building seems to have been made possible by the fact that Cordero won several lottery prizes, and it is said that his winnings reached a sum so great that the Spanish Treasury, lacking the necessary liquidity, was forced to grant him land instead. Others maintain that he didn't win any lottery, but enjoyed close connections with the Spanish administration, allowing him to acquire the site. First occupied by the monastery of San Felipe el Real (from 1546), it became a prime location once the city of Madrid began to expand in the mid nineteenth century. The lottery anecdote was merely a way of justifying his acquisition.

Casa Cordero, designed by architect Juan José Sánchez Pescador, occupies an entire city block and is often cited as exemplary for its simplicity and functional character: its dwellings are adapted to various economic and social profiles. For this reason, it is considered to be the first purpose-built residential building in the city. It also contains a renowned guesthouse called Casa Vizcaina, in tribute to its original owner, a native of the Basque province of Vizcaya.

GUIDED TOUR OF THE MADRID ATHENAEUM ⑫

Calle del Prado, 21
- www.ateneodemadrid.com
- Appointment on request: 91 429 17 50
- Guided tours: Monday–Friday from 10am to 1pm (by appointment only)
- Length of tours: 45 to 60 minutes • Admission: €2
- Metro: Antón Martín or Sevilla

> *Where it was concluded that God does not exist*

Founded in 1835, the Ateneo de Madrid is the oldest cultural institution in Spain as well as a very special place in its own right, with pre-booked guided tours (lasting approximately an hour). These fascinating tours not only reveal a number of anecdotes associated with the Ateneo but also provide explanations of the place's numerous Masonic symbols (see following page) and information about the history of the building and of each of its various rooms: the Annals Hall (Salon de los Actos), the vestibule, the portrait gallery, the Sala de la Cacherreria and the office of Manuel Azaña. The library is not included in the tour, but there is another way to visit it (see p. 139).

The Annals Hall (see p. 137), with its decor inspired by Masonic motifs and symbols, is also one of the first expressions of modernism in Madrid. And it was in this room that in 1932, when Spain was a staunchly Catholic state, the conclusion was reached that God does not exist – a verdict that caused a great international scandal. It was also here that impassioned speeches in defence of freedom were made by the likes of Ortega y Gasset (on return from exile) and receptions held in honour of such figures as Einstein, Madame Curie and Mother Teresa.

The Portrait Gallery has an exceptional collection of works by the major Spanish painters of recent centuries, as well as a wide-ranging display of visual material relating to the cultural and political life of the nineteenth and twentieth centuries. On one of the walls you can see the now-bricked-in doorway that used to lead directly through to the Chamber of Deputies. It was once said that what could not be discussed in the Chamber could always be readily debated here in the Ateneo (in particular within the Sala de la Cacharreria, which became a legendary "talking shop").

Manuel Azaña's office stands next to the Portrait Gallery. In this room, at dawn on 17 July 1936, there was a breakdown in negotiations that ultimately led to the Spanish Civil War.

The first premises of the Ateneo de Madrid were a much more modest affair in Calle Montera; the present building in Calle del Prado was built, to designs by Luis Landecho and Enrique Fort, in 1884 and officially opened by Cánovas Del Castillo and King Alfonso XII. Since its foundation, the Athenaeum has been a champion of cultural liberty and freedom of thought, promoting conferences, debates and discussions.

MADRID'S ATHENAEUM: CULTURE AND ESOTERICISM

The Ateneo Científico, Literario y Artístico de Madrid was created to promote a liberal movement in Spain that would defend freedom of thought and expression.

This objective was in accord with the ideology of Freemasonry and theosophy also practised by a majority of the Athenaeum's founders. Various signs of this affiliation can be seen in the building.

Prior to the Spanish Civil War (1936–1939), there were paintings on the walls of the Athenaeum representing allegories and symbols that alluded to Freemasonry and theosophy, although a great many of them were destroyed after the conflict by the Francoist regime.

Other works were successfully hidden, as was revealed once restoration work was carried out. Thus, one will note the fresco showing the painter's palette with Masonic instruments such as the square and mallet, but also drawings composed of three images: a column (symbol of the union between the Earth and the Heavens), an owl (symbol of wisdom), and a lamp (symbol of the Athenaeum) representing the Seed, the Development and the Purpose in the Masonic world.

Camouflaged doors, which at first sight seem to be merely part of the decor, actually give access to secret passages.

The door in the portrait gallery thus leads to the Congreso de los Diputados (lower house of the Spanish Parliament), although it is now sealed off. Others take you to unexpected spots within the Athenaeum itself: one passage ends near the stairway with the statue of the "Vanquished Warrior", a work by Agustín Querol, here representing Mercury (Hermes) brandishing a large broken sword in his left hand, while his right hand holds a statuette of the goddess Minerva (Athena), symbolising wisdom overcoming constraint.

The five-pointed Masonic star that adorned the table where the most important rites were celebrated, as well as the majority of stars on the stairways, were destroyed in the 1960s, following a complaint by the right-wing newspaper, *ABC*.

In the Reception Room and the English Room, in addition to works by Enrique Mélida (1834–1892) and Karen Petrus Cornelius de Basel (1869–1923), both Freemasons and members of the theosophical movement, five-pointed stars on the backs of the chairs attest to the founders' Masonic connections.

On the building's façade, you can also see the Lamp of Wisdom as well as stars that were later re-carved and transformed into flowers.

In addition to Manuel Azaña and Mario Roso de Luna (see p. 238), the institution also included among its members a circle of theosophers and Freemasons of a progressive bent, such as Augusto Barcia, Fernando de los Ríos, Viriato Díaz Pérez, Tomás Doreste, and the painter Rafael Monleón Moret, who created some of the works that decorate the premises.

Another famous member was the doctor and Freemason Simorra, of whom it is said that he permitted his patients to be interned at the Athenaeum, a rumour which gave rise to wild tales about goings-on inside.

Another celebrity was the librarian Rafael Urbano, an expert in demonology, whose funeral wake was held at the Athenaeum.

ANNALS HALL IN THE ATENEO DE MADRID ⓭

Calle del Prado, 21
- www.ateneodemadrid.com
- Phone for an appointment: 91 429 17 50
- Guided tours: Monday–Friday from 10am to 1pm (by appointment only)
- Length of tours: 45 minutes • Admission: €2
- Metro: Antón Martín or Sevilla

> **One of the first examples of modernism in Madrid**

This Sala de los Actos is the most interesting part of the Ateneo de Madrid (see p. 133); a pioneering work by Artura Mélida, it is one of the first examples of modernism (Art Nouveau) in Madrid.

The sumptuous decoration expresses the *raison d'être* and function of the Athenaeum. The ceiling, with a surface area of 200 square metres, is decorated at its centre with a small Greek temple housing three mythological figures: Hermes, Athena and Apollo, the three gods of Olympus who were associated with Wisdom.

The drapery about to fall behind Apollo allows a glimpse of the Sun, represented by Apollo's own chariot, with the god being responsible for riding across the firmament in order to drive back night and place the Sun at the highest point in the heavens. This is a scene in which light symbolises the "enlightened" individual.

Around these figures are twelve tableaux or allegories that depict both the Twelve Labours of Hercules and the Signs of the Zodiac. Revealing great harmony of palette and line, these images combine theosophical doctrine and Masonic symbolism. At the foot of the temple, a colourful decorative work – complete with dragon, rising sun and ibis (a symbol of eternity) – seems to express a link with the world of the East, with the Japan that so fascinated nineteenth-century Europe.

Around this central motif are references to the twelve sections that made up the Athenaeum in 1884 (Literature, Mathematics, Eloquence, etc.). Each is symbolised by the silhouette of a magnificently well-rounded female form.

Around the podium there are also three pretty panels that refer to the main activities of the Athenaeum: Science (associated here with Arab culture), Literature (associated with Classical Rome) and Art (associated with Christian culture).

On the Masonic and theosophical symbols in the *Sala de los Actos*, see the previous double page.

PECERA LIBRARY

Ateneo de Madrid
Calle del Prado, 21
• www.ateneodemadrid.com
• Metro: Antón Martín or Sevilla
• Booking: 91 531 40 18 / 657 847 685 • correo@carpetaniamadrid.com
• For membership: send a letter with reason for application and CV. You
must be sponsored by three members and pay an enrolment fee of €110.

> *Where Donoso Cortes was born and Moreno Nieto died, where Cánovas lost his sight and Castelar his hair*

Once a month the *Carpetania Madrid* Association holds a nocturnal walk through the Barrio de las Lettras (Literature Quarter) which includes a visit to the Athenaeum and entry to its library, known colloquially as *La Pecera* (The Aquarium). This is the only way you can gain access to this magnificent library without being an Ateneo member.

Originally, the library occupied just one room – the one now known as *La Pecera*; a place with a wonderful atmosphere, this was frequented by all the great Spanish intellectuals and Nobel prizewinners.

In 1910 refurbishment work began, with the library being extended to incorporate the two rooms alongside, thus creating a general room which was then used exclusively as a reading room.

Tradition has it that Donoso Cortes was born here, Cánovas lost his sight and Castelar his hair, and Moreno Nieto died here – which gives some idea of the illustrious figures who have frequented this library.

The library collection itself stretches back to sixteenth-century publications, with books either from donations and bequests by members or from a Royal Decree of 1838. This decree was intended to enrich the library by directing donations to it from the National Print Works, the Library of Parliament, the National Library and from the libraries of the various monasteries and convents that had closed down. The result is a collection of extraordinary variety and quality – particularly with regard to nineteenth-century material. One of the curiosities of the collection is the number of books from the USSR and the Third Reich; these are here as a result of exchanges made with the Republican government and the Franco regime during the 1930s.

SOCIEDAD CERVANTINA PRESS

Calle Atocha, 87
• Tel: 91 420 3437
• Open Monday–Thursday from 9.30am to 1.30pm and 3pm to 7pm;
Friday 9.30am to 1.30pm
• Metro: Atocha

> **The building
> where
> Don Quixote
> was printed**

A plaque at No. 87 Calle Atocha identifies the place where Miguel de Cervantes' masterpiece *Don Quixote* was first printed. Listed since 1981, the building has since 1955 been the premises of the Sociedad Cervantina, founded two years earlier. Long before, it had housed the old printworks of Juan de la Cuesta.

Along with collections of bibliographical material relating to Cervantes' work, there is also a wooden replica of the press used by Juan de la Cuesta himself in printing the first edition of *Don Quixote*; visitors are even allowed to operate it, so as to get some idea of how an old printing press worked. Conferences are also held here, and there is a project for the building of a small chamber theatre for productions of plays dating from the *Siglo de Oro* (Golden Age of Spanish literature).

It was Francisco de Robles, a well-respected bookseller, who purchased the manuscript of *Don Quixote* in 1604, turning to the printworks of Pedro Madrigal (then run by his son-in-law, Juan de la Cuesta) for the publication of the book. The first part of *El ingenioso hidalgo Don Quijote de la Mancha* came out in 1605, with a mass of printing errors due to the haste imposed by the terms of the contract. Furthermore, the overall quality of the edition was rather poor: the paper from El Paular monastery was coarse and the typeface was crude. Still, Robles had invested a total of 8,000 *reales* in producing

the book, of which 1,500 went to Cervantes himself, and Juan de la Cuesta went on to produce a second, corrected, edition that same year.

As well as *Don Quixote*, the printer produced Cervantes' other books and numerous now-classic texts of the *Siglo de Oro* – including Lope de Vega's *Las almenas de toro* (The Bull Battlements) and *Los amantes sin amor* (Loveless Lovers). With its total of six presses operated by twenty workers, his printworks also produced various official documents for the Crown.

CALLE DE LA CABEZA

PLAQUE IN CALLE DE LA CABEZA

Calle de la Cabeza, corner of Calle Lavapiés
• Metro: Tirso de Molina or Sol

*A dark
legend*

I n the old city centre the street signs are often *azulejos*, complete with illustrations that bear some relation to the street name. In the case of Calle de la Cabeza that illustration is a terrifying image of a severed head on a silver platter.

Legend has it that a priest who used to live in this street had a servant who was so ambitious that he ultimately murdered his employer in order to seize his gold. Having killed the cleric, the servant cut off his head then disappeared to Portugal. Days passed and the street's inhabitants began to notice the absence of the priest. Finally, the heinous crime was discovered by a parishioner, who went into the house when a message came from the parish of San Sebastian requesting the priest for a burial service.

Many years later, the servant, who in the meantime had transformed himself into a gentleman, returned to Madrid. Happening to be in the area of the Rastro street market one day, he bought a lamb's head. A police officer, however, later noticed that blood was dripping from the bag he was carrying and stopped him: "What have you got there?" "A lamb's head," the ex-servant answered confidently. However, when the bag was opened, the policeman was horrified to find the head of the murdered priest.

The servant was condemned to death by hanging, whilst Philip III honoured the dead cleric by having a stone head set in place on the façade of what had been his house. Years later the local inhabitants decided to remove that head so they could forget the tragedy. In exchange, they built a chapel in honour of the Virgin of Carmen, which was the origin of the Penitential Order of Our Lady of Carmen.

INQUISITION DUNGEON

Until just a few years ago, in the Taverna del Avapiés at the corner of this street, there were traces of an Inquisition dungeon. The building, however, was practically a ruin and the *taverna* was obliged to close.

MASONIC SYMBOLISM AT THE MINISTRY

Ministry of Agriculture
Paseo de la Infante Isabel, 1
• Metro: Antocha

The work of Masonic architects

Designed by the architect and Freemason Ricardo Velázquez Bosco (1843–1923), the building that now houses the Spanish Ministry of Agriculture, Fisheries and Food was completed in 1897. Originally occupied by the Ministry of Development, it displays numerous Masonic references on its main façade.

On either side of the front entrance stand two gigantic caryatids representing Commerce and Industry. The Commerce statue carries a mallet (emblem of the venerable Master Mason invested with authority) and the square (symbol of Masonic rectitude). The Industry statue bears a cogwheel (symbol of progress), sheaves of wheat (symbol of abundance), and the caduceus of Mercury whose entwined black and white serpents signify Life and Death.

Above, on the intermediate floor, is a terrace with eight Corinthian columns. Arranged in pairs, they recall the two columns of the Temple of Solomon in Jerusalem (*Jachin* and *Boaz*), symbols of union and balance, of Heaven and Earth, of the Sun and the Moon, of light and of fire, of the creator and the creation, which are supported by the strength of the Great Architect of the Universe.

In Masonic symbolism, the three types of temple columns (Doric, Ionic and Corinthian) symbolise not only the three persons of the Trinity (represented by the Luminous Delta or Triangle with the Eye of Providence at its centre), but also the three highest officers in a Masonic lodge:

> Doric – father – Worshipful Master
> Ionic – mother – Senior Warden
> Corinthian – son – Junior Warden

The top of the building is crowned by a group of sculptures entitled *La Gloria y los Pegasos* (The Glory and the Pegasus), an allegory of universal progress commissioned from the Catalan sculptor Agustí Querol i Subirats (1860–1909), who was a high-ranking Freemason. Here we see Glory offering palms and laurels to Art and Science. At her side, two groups of Pegasus (winged horses) in bronze are guided by the spirits of Agriculture and Industry (to the left) and Philosophy and Letters (to the right).

The three figures in the central group are allusions to the Grand National Lodge of Spain, which in Spanish Masonic circles, is the only legitimate body in possession of the Three Pillars of Freemasonry (Wisdom, Strength and

Beauty), embodied by three moral sources of light: the book of the law (the Bible, Koran, Veda, etc. according to the rite and the country), the square, and the compass.

The book bears the wisdom which is the glory of the Master Mason. The square is the strength of the journeyman Mason's art which transforms and uplifts nature into its highest form. The compass indicates the beauty inherent in the science which the apprentice Mason gradually learns.

Agustí Querol composed this set of sculptures in 1905, based on elements from classical Greco-Roman mythology, to reflect a global vision of progress (the fundamental allegorical concept), on a material and social level as well as a mental and spiritual plane. The figure three, a number cherished by Freemasonry, is present throughout the set, which is distributed in three parts, themselves divided into three groups, each composed of three allegorical figures.

LAS ESCUELAS PÍAS LIBRARY

Calle Sombrerete, 15
• Tel: 91 467 5843
• Open Monday–Friday from 9.30am to 9pm
• Special visits from 8pm to 9pm
• Metro: Lavapiés

*On
the ruins
of the church*

The library of the Escuelas Pías de l'Universidad Nacional de Educación a Distancia (UNED, National University of Distance Learning) was, rather amazingly, built upon the ruins of the Escuelas Pías de San Fernando church. For years, these ruins had been nothing but an unofficial rubbish tip, then – over the period 1996 to 1999 – the architect J.I. Linazasoro undertook the complicated project of restoring and refurbishing the ruins to create a nine-storey building. Despite the total transformation of the site, the characteristic feature of the school – the immense rounded arch surmounted by the crest of the original Escuelas Pias – has been preserved; it is through this that you enter a rotunda of eight columns supporting a magnificent cupola.

The Escuelas Pias, founded in 1729, was the first school in Madrid run by the Order of the Piarists (*Escolapios*). It provided education for children from poor backgrounds, and was also considered revolutionary for its day because it set up the first school in Spain specifically for deaf-mutes.

The ruins on which the present-day library was built were those of the school church, built in 1763–1791 to designs by Friar Gabriel Escribano and destroyed in 1936 during the Civil War, when arson and pillage reduced the school to a bare skeleton. After the Civil War a cinema was installed here, and there was a plan (never implemented) to turn the whole site into a public garden.

To gain admission to the library and reading rooms, you must have a user pass. These are provided free; just bring your passport/identity card and two photographs. The facilities are open to those interested between 8pm and 9pm, or by appointment (arranged by phone).

CAFÉ WITH A VIEW

The Café Gaudeamus is an amazing place. For a modest price you can relax in a deckchair, enjoying your drink while looking out over magnificent views of south Madrid. The café owes its name to the famous university hymn *Gaudeamus igitur* ("So let us rejoice"), which dates back to the thirteenth century. It is on the terrace of the library of the Escuelas Pias library; access, free of charge, is by the same entrance as the library (No. 15 Calle Sombrerete).

MUSEO DE FARMACIA MILITAR

Calle Embajadores, 75
• Tel: 91 527 36 23
• Open Tuesdays and Thursdays, from 10.00 to 12 noon
• Admission free; call in advance for an appointment
• Metro: Embajadores

**Medications
by alchemy**

One of most surprising rooms in the little-known but interesting Museum of Military Pharmacy is the iatrochemical laboratory (iatrochemistry was a school of medical thought which attempted to explain physiological mechanisms through chemical reactions), which was installed more than 300 years ago in the cellar of the Royal Pharmacy and transferred here for display.

In this laboratory, and at the express request of the Spanish king, attempts were made to obtain medications by alchemy. As Spain had no specialists in the field of iatrochemistry, in 1693 King Charles followed the advice of his viceroy in Naples who sent him Vito Cotaldo, a prestigious Italian pharmacist, so that the latter could carry out experiments on preparations that he would subsequently prescribe to the king's troops.

In the other rooms of the museum, you can see items retracing the evolution of the scientific equipment used by military pharmacists: photos of the machines that turned out pills and suppositories, and a laboratory from the 1940s with a very complete collection of test tubes, scales and ovens from the period. The case displaying drugs derived from plants and animals

is astonishing: in all, there are over 400 varieties of psychotropic substances, most of them originating in former Spanish colonies.

The museum was founded in 1928 with the aim of gathering materials from various military facilities involved in the research and fabrication of medications. The building dates from 1915 and was commissioned by the Spanish Army to house the central laboratory for the military health service. The construction was directed by the military engineer Pascual Fernández Aceituno.

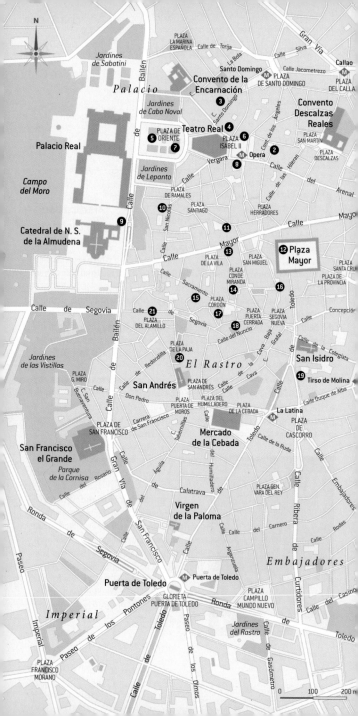

CENTRE-WEST

THE PRIVATE COLLECTION OF "AQUARIUM MADRID"

①

Maestro Victoria, 8
• Open Monday–Saturday, 11am to 2pm and 5pm to 9pm. Sundays and bank holidays, 12pm to 2.30pm and 5pm to 9pm
• Admission: children €2; adults €4
• Metro: Sol

Wild animals in the centre of Madrid

Near Puerta del Sol, the "Aquarium Madrid" pet shop houses a surprising collection in the basement. Just follow the stairs down to be transported into a sort of small zoo where the animals stare at the visitors from the shelter of their glass cages.

Visitors are rather rare, especially on weekdays, as most customers only come to the store to buy pet supplies. So you can generally have the place all to yourself, which of course makes the visit all the more interesting.

Some of the animals are particularly impressive, such as the boa constrictor, the dwarf crocodile whose snout has a remarkable deformity, the European fire-bellied toad, the emperor scorpion, or the giant millipede 30 centimetres long and as thick as a thumb. As for the red snake, he might just give you a scare when you see him uncoil out of the shadows.

On the main floor, you can also find all sorts of pet products as well as fish for sale at a modest sum (€2 and up).

ORATORY OF SANTO NIÑO DEL REMEDIO   ❷

Calle de los Donados, 6
• Open Monday—Sunday from 8am to 12 noon and 6pm to 8pm
• Metro: Ópera

Statue of a miracle-working child

The unassuming oratory of Santo Niño del Remedio (Holy Child of Healing) contains a little statue of a child that is venerated as having miracle-working properties.

The story dates back to the nineteenth century, when a lady of the city's *haute bourgeoisie* decided to sell off some of her possessions, among which was a statue of the Infant Jesus. This was bought for just 5 pesetas by the bookbinder Pedro Martín Mazarruela, who placed the "child" in his workshop at No. 4 Calle de Costanilla de los Ángeles. Every evening the Mazzaruela family would gather to pray to the Infant Jesus, also making clothes for the statue. Gradually the number of fervent devotees increased – undoubtedly because of rumours of miracles and because a secret visit to the statue had been paid by Queen María Cristina, mother of Alfonso XIII, who was seeking the strength to bear both her state of widowhood and the responsibilities of regent.

With the help of modest donations from the faithful, the bookbinder's shop became an improvised chapel. Up to that point the statue had not had a name, and it was decided to choose one by drawing lots: the words "hope", "pardon" and "healing" (*remedio*) were written on pieces of paper, from which a priest drew just one – thus the child became the *Santo Niño del Remedio*.

The present-day sculpture has undergone various restorations – for example, glass eyes have been added, as have eyebrows that heighten the expressive power of the face. The foot, damaged by the numerous kisses of the faithful, has also been restored; the feet are now protected by little silver slippers.

On the 13th of every month, the *Santo Niño del Remedio* is placed in a crib for veneration by the faithful.

CREST AND INSCRIPTION CARVED IN STONE – EVIDENCE OF DAYS LONG GONE ...

The oratory was built in 1917 on the site of the old church of the Hospital of Santa Catalina de los Donados, which itself had been founded in 1460 by Pedro Fernández de Lorca, treasurer to King Juan II and secretary to King Enrique IV (Henry IV of Castile), who intended it as a hospice for twelve elderly invalids. The *Donados* in the street name refers to the garments worn by those twelve old men, who paid special veneration to St Catherine without however taking holy orders; they also offered prayers every day for the soul of the benefactor who had founded the hospice. The hospice later became a hospital for the blind, before being demolished in the nineteenth century. An inscription in stone within the oratory bears witness to that period and recalls the date on which Fernández Lorca founded the hospice. There is also a crest which was preserved when the old building was demolished.

LIQUEFACTION OF THE BLOOD
OF ST PANTALEON

❸

Real Monasterio de La Encarnación
Plaza de la Encarnación, 1
• Tel: 91 542 69 47
• Open Tuesday, Wednesday, Thursday and Saturday from 10.30am to
12.45pm and 4pm to 5.45pm; Friday 10.30am to 12.45pm; Sundays and
holidays 11am to 1.45pm
• Admission: €3.60
• Metro: Ópera

"

*Miracle
of St Pantaleon*

O nce a year, on 27 July, the blood of
St Pantaleon contained in a reliquary
in the church of the Real Monasterio
de La Encarnación (Royal Monastery of the
Incarnation) liquefies, turning from a solid to a liquid state.

The church itself has never confirmed nor denied this "miracle of
St Pantaleon". However, tradition has it that – just as with the blood of
San Gennaro (St Januarius, patron saint of Naples) – the non-occurrence
of the liquefaction is a sign of future catastrophe: for example, this is what
happened in 1914 (before the First World War) and in 1936 (before the
Spanish Civil War).

Until 1993 the faithful were actually allowed to kiss the reliquary that
contains the blood, but this was then forbidden because of the states of
exaltation it could produce and the damage caused to the reliquary itself.
Nowadays, the "miracle" is broadcast on closed-circuit television monitors
specially installed for the occasion.

The reliquary itself initially belonged to the Vatican, but was presented by
Pope Paul V to Juan de Zuñiga, Spanish viceroy in Naples, in 1661, who then
gave it to the Real Monasterio de La Encarnación when his own daughter,
Mariana de Jesus, became a nun at the convent there.

As well as this blood, the convent possesses other reliquaries of great
importance to the faithful. These include the arms of eight martyrs, the leg of
St Margaret, part of the back of St Thomas of Villanueva, an arm of St Isabella
and numerous other relics, all contained in 700 reliquaries.

MIRACLE OR MERELY A PHYSICAL PHENOMENON?

Many doubt the veracity of this miracle and of those associated with the
same saint in Rome (see *Secret Rome* in this series of guides) and with
San Gennaro in Naples. Some have even mixed together a compound
which behaves in the same way as the supposedly miraculous blood.
Made using ingredients that were all available during the Middle Ages —
egg yolk, kitchen salt, iron carbonate — the solution is very dense but, due
to a physical property known as thixotropy, liquefies when shaken. As
happens with the blood of St Pantaleon, this mixture tends to work on most
occasions ... sometimes liquefying immediately, sometimes slowly, but
sometimes not at all.

PANTALEON: A POSSESSOR OF HERMETIC WISDOM?

The life of Pantaleon – whose name means "resembling a lion in everything" – appears in the *Acta Santorum* (Acts of the Saints) written by the eighteenth-century Belgian Jesuit Jean Bolland. He says that Pantaleon was born in the third century AD, son of Eustorgius and Eubula, in the city of Nicomedia (modern-day Izmit, in Turkey). Like his father he was a physician, but he was also a philosopher known to the nobility and the royal court of Byzantium. Pantaleon converted to his mother's religion of Christianity but was imprisoned during the Diocletian persecution of the Church and condemned to death. He was beheaded in public on 27 July 305. Tradition has it that the Christians of Nicomedia soaked up his blood with bits of cotton that they then kept in small glass phials, which were later distributed as veneration of the saint spread to Italy, France and Spain.

It is not known exactly how, but Pantaleon figures in the lineage of the first Christian initiates – the possessors of Gnostic wisdom. This wisdom is also known as "hermetic", after the Greek god Hermes, and the Christian priest who is said to have initiated Pantaleon and his two disciples, Hermippes and Hermocrates, was actually called Hermolaüs. All four men were beheaded together, but it was Pantaleon who was bound to an olive tree outside the city. He is also said to have made the swords of his executioners blush. When his head rolled to the ground, the blood that soaked into the olive tree is said to have made the tree flower and immediately produce fruit. Symbolically, that episode signifies the flourishing of the *Pax Ecclesia* (the olive tree is a symbol of peace) within the lands of Asia Minor as a result of St Pantaleon's work in spreading the Gospels and his death as a martyr.

The wisdom of the initiate Pantaleon is reflected in the prodigious feats he performed. First, he overcame a serpent (the symbolic guardian of secret knowledge) then restored the sight of his blind father. He also suffered a sequence of different torments, which themselves denote a gradual initiation into higher knowledge. The presence of "three Hermes" – Hermippes, Hermocrates and Hermolaüs – within Pantaleon's prison cell suggests a link with Hermes Trismegistus, confirming the illumination that the sage received after overcoming the difficult trials that he underwent before achieving the level of "master". Then comes the final act in his martyrdom, with the saint tied to an olive tree – the religious plant *par excellence* in the Mediterranean region. And the fact that his blood makes the tree flower and bear fruit – that is, nurtures a renewal of faith – is evidently a symbolic reference to Christ's own sacrifice. Indeed, this miraculous blood of St Pantaleon links him directly with the Western tradition of the Holy Grail, which contained Christ's blood.

It is also interesting to note that the relic of St Pantaleon came from the Romanesque church of San Pantaleon in the Vale de Losa near Burgos in north-east Castile – known as an enclave of traditional magic. It is no coincidence that the names of various places nearby recall the word "grail": a little to the north is the village of Criales (*Griales* or *Grial* in Castilian) and, close to the frontier with the Basque country, is Sierra Salvada, which clearly parallels the Montsalvat mentioned in the Grail poem *Parzival* by Wolfram von Eschenbach (c. 1170–1220).

THE CULT OF CHRISTIAN RELICS

Although rather neglected these days, with their devoted following greatly diminished in numbers, saints' relics had extraordinary success from the Middle Ages onwards. Their presence today in numerous churches across Europe is a reminder of those exceptional times.

The cult of Christian relics goes back to the beginning of Christianity, to the deaths of the early martyrs and the creation of the first saints. The function of these relics was threefold: they bore witness to the example of a righteous and virtuous life to be copied or followed; they possessed a spiritual energy and power that could even work miracles (it was believed that the miraculous powers of the saints themselves was retained by their relics); and over time, with the rise of the contested practice of granting indulgences, relics bestowed indulgences on those who possessed them (see opposite).

As demand dictated supply, it was not long before unscrupulous parties were competing to invent their own relics, aided in their task by the Church which, for political reasons, canonised a great number of undeserving individuals (see opposite). Over-production went to absurd extremes: if the authenticity of all their relics was to be accepted, Mary

Magdalene would have had six bodies, and St. Biagio a hundred arms.

These excesses, of course, raised suspicions and the popularity of relics gradually waned, although many people still believe that the true relic of a saint possesses spiritual power. How else can the numerous pilgrimages in the footsteps of Father Pio throughout Italy be explained?

There are around 50,000 relics scattered around Europe, from some 5,000 saints.

Note that most of the world's other religions also worship relics, or used to do so.

21,441 RELICS FOR 39,924,120 YEARS OF INDULGENCES!

The greatest collector of relics was Frederick III of Saxony (1463-1525), who procured 21,441 of them in all, 42 of which were fully preserved bodies of saints. Based on this unique collection, he calculated that he had amassed a grand total of 39,924,120 years and 220 days of indulgences! However, under the influence of Luther, who opposed indulgences, he abandoned the cult of relics in 1523.

WHEN SAINTS ARE NOT SO HOLY: ST. GEORGE, ST. CHRISTOPHER, AND ST. PHILOMENA, STRUCK FROM THE LIST...

From the Middle Ages onwards, the pursuit of relics continued, as did their falsification. Not only relics were fabricated, however. Sometimes, even the saints themselves were a fabrication.

Recently – an event that passed almost without comment – the Church purged St. George, St. Christopher and St. Philomena from its calendar, the very existence of all three now being in doubt.

The totally abusive canonisation of certain real personalities also took place, allowing the objects connected with them to feed the market for saintly relics.

For diplomatic reasons linked to the Counter-Reformation of the 16th century, canonisation was often based on political rather than religious or moral criteria. As a result of this *Realpolitik*, many rulers of the time were thus sanctified in a bid to ensure their subjects' allegiance to the Roman Catholic Church, then under pressure from the Protestant movement. St. Stanislas of Poland, St. Casimir of Lithuania, St. Brigitte of Sweden, St. Stephen of Hungary, St. Margaret of Scotland, St. Elizabeth of Portugal, St. Wenceslas of Bohemia ... The list is long, indeed.

RELICS OF THE FEATHERS OF THE ARCHANGEL MICHAEL, THE BREATH OF JESUS, AND EVEN THE STARLIGHT THAT GUIDED THE THREE WISE MEN!

Leaving no stone unturned in their efforts to make money at the expense of the most naive believers, relic merchants showed unparalleled imagination in their quest for sacred paraphernalia and invented some fascinating objects, such as the horns of Moses or the feathers of the Archangel Michael, recorded as having been on sale at Mont-Saint-Michel in 1784.

The most highly prized relics were of course those of Christ. Unfortunately for relic hunters, as Christ had ascended to Heaven, his body was by definition no longer on Earth. Imagination again came to the rescue in the form of the quite extraordinary relic of the breath of Jesus (!) which was preserved in Wittenberg cathedral, Germany, in a glass phial.

The remains of Christ's foreskin, recuperated after his circumcision seven days after birth, and of his umbilical cord (!) were preserved at Latran, Rome (in the Sancta Sanctorum) while bread from the Last Supper was kept at Gaming, Austria. Certain medieval texts lost to us today even spoke of the relic of the rays of the star that guided the Wise Men, also preserved at Latran.

REAL ACADEMIA NACIONAL DE MEDICINA LIBRARY

❹

Calle Arrieta, 12
• Metro: Ópera
• Tel: 91 547 0318
• Although you can visit the library without an appointment, we recommend phoning first
• Scientific debates are held on Tuesdays at 6pm
• www.ranm.es

A very special private library

The pretty little library on the second floor of the Royal Academy of Medicine is a charming place, largely unknown to Madrilenes themselves. The steel-framed interior with floor-to-ceiling windows contains around 100,000 medical books and long reading tables under the muted light of classic reading lamps with green shades.

In the adjoining room is a section with gynaecology texts donated by Dr José Botellat, as well as the older parts of the collection (with books that date back to the sixteenth century).

The building – complete with a doorway flanked by two figures of Atlas – was constructed in 1913 to designs by the architect María Cabello Lapiedra. However, La Real Academia de Medicina was founded much earlier, by a group of physicians who in the 1730s began to hold meetings in various homes and coffee shops, and even in the pharmacy run by one of the group, José Ortega. Set up with the purpose of promoting scientific research, the group referred to itself as the Madrid Literary Medicinal Assembly (Tertulia Literaria Médica Matritense). In 1734 they applied for the patronage of King Philip V, choosing as their emblematic figurehead the ancient Greek Archimedes, an inventor, scientist and mathematician who is said to have sunk the Roman fleet by using a series of parabolic mirrors to focus the heat of the Sun's rays upon it. Although royal patronage was forthcoming, the group still had to wait a further 200 years before they obtained their own meeting place (built on the site previously occupied by the National Library).

The Academy not only offers visitors the chance to see the library and the exhibition space in the main hall, it also holds public scientific debates every Tuesday. During these sessions, the academicians are seated in the fifty different chairs that represent the various fields of medical specialisation. The hall in which these events are held has a magnificent glass ceiling.

REINANDO

ISABEL SEGUNDA

DE BORBON

AÑO DE

THE TAIL OF PHILIP IV'S HORSE ⑤

Sculpture that defies the laws of engineering

Officially inaugurated in 1843, but designed in 1632, the equestrian statue of Philip IV was the first sculpture in the world to defy the laws of engineering. Its designer, Italian sculptor Pietro Tacca, based his work on drawings by Velázquez and the desires of Philip IV, who wanted his statue to set a worldwide artistic precedent. To that purpose, he chose a pose defying the laws of gravity in which the horse rears up and stands on its hind legs only. In order to evenly distribute the weight of the statue, the Italian sculptor turned to Galileo, who advised the artist to make the hindquarters in solid metal while leaving the front of the statue hollow. He also suggested that the horse could discreetly lean on its tail.

WHY ARE THE STATUES IN PLAZA DE ORIENTE SET DIRECTLY ON THE GROUND?

If, as you can clearly see, the sculptures of the twenty Spanish kings in Plaza de Oriente are set directly on the ground, it's because they should have graced the upper cornice of the Royal Palace.

According to popular legend, the wife of Ferdinand VI, Barbara of Braganza, dreamed that the statues fell from the cornice of the Royal Palace on a stormy night, thus causing much damage.

So the king decided that these statues carved in limestone were not to be placed on the cornice.

Another theory simply has it that Charles III, who didn't care for the Baroque style of the statues, ordered them to be removed, according to a royal decree dated 8 February 1760.

NEARBY

THE WELL ST DOMINIC DUG WITH HIS OWN HANDS ⑥

No. 3 Calle Campomanes stands on the very spot where St Dominic de Guzmán dug a well with his own hands, from 1218 to 1219, to supply water for the nuns of the neighbouring convent. The water that gushed from this well was hailed as miraculous because it was believed to cure disease. The well, partially destroyed in the Peninsular War, was replaced in 1840. Today, all that remains are some vestiges in a residential building that unfortunately isn't open to visitors, unless you know someone who lives in the building or can successfully convince the guardian to let you in.

VESTIGES OF A MUSLIM TOWER IN PLAZA DE ORIENTE CAR PARK ❼

Plaza de Oriente s/n

> ❝ **A car park filled with history**

Madrid conceals its archaeological ruins in some rather unexpected places. For example, you can find vestiges of the Muslim Torre de los Huesos (Tower of Bones) in the car park on Plaza de Oriente, away from the tourist circuits. The tower, or what remains of it, was discovered in 1996 during the construction of the car park and is now protected behind glass.

Torre de los Huesos, named for its proximity to the Islamic "Huesa de Raf" cemetery, was a Muslim watchtower that stood outside the city and served as a defensive hold. At the end of the ninth century, when King Alfonso VI of Castile conquered Madrid, the watchtower was incorporated within the new Christian city wall and served to protect the Valnadú gate, one of the four entrances that existed at the time.

In the car park, one level down, you can also see reproductions of different items, mainly jars, discovered at the foot of the wall.

THE MUSLIM WALL

Madrid's first wall stretched over 4 hectares and dated from the end of the ninth century. Its perimeter ran within the Plaza de la Armería (at the corner of Calle Mayor and Calle de Bailén), the Palacio Uceda, Cuesta de la Vega and Almudena Cathedral. The best-preserved vestiges of the wall that protected Mayrit, the Muslim city that later became Madrid, can be found near Almudena Cathedral, in Cuesta de la Vega. These vestiges were part of the first fortress and were integrated into the gardens of Emir Mohamed I. The wall served to protect the Alcázar, which stood on the present site of the Royal Palace and which was strategically located to defend the road to Toledo that belonged to the Caliphate of Córdoba.

WALK AROUND THE REMAINS OF THE CHRISTIAN CITY WALLS

8

> *The medieval wall that has survived through time*

After Alfonso VI's conquest of Madrid in the eleventh century, the walls of the Muslim citadel were extended, with what are known as the "Christian Walls" embracing a wider perimeter.

This second ring of walls enclosed an area of just over 33 hectares, meeting up with the Arab walls in the area of Cuesta de la Vega. The layout of the new wall followed a course that would today run through Plaza del Humilladero, along Calle de la Cava Baja to Porta Cerrada and then across Calle Mayor (in the area of Calle del Espejo and Calle de la Escalminata) towards the Ópera district, meeting up with the Alcazar in the area of Plaza de Oriente. With the removal of the court to Madrid in 1561, the city expanded beyond the walls, various parts of which were demolished. However some stretches were incorporated into new buildings, which means that part of the walls has survived to this day.

At Nos. 15–17 Calle del Almendro is another stretch of surviving wall in a small garden that can be seen from the street. Finally, at No. 3 Plaza de Ópera, the cellar of a restaurant contains part of the medieval walls, obviously only accessible during the restaurant opening hours.

ORIGINS OF THE MADRID *PUERTAS*

The Puerta de Alcalá, Puerta de Toledo and Puerta del Sol are all city gateways whose locations reflect how the five successive rings of walls around Madrid changed as the city expanded eastwards. However, the last three rings were not defensive fortifications, as the so-called Muslim and Christian walls had been, but rather customs barriers which might also serve in cases of quarantine; they were known as the Cerca de los Arrabales (thirteenth century), Cerca de Felipe II (sixteenth century) and Cerca de Felipe IV (seventeenth to eighteenth centuries). Very few of the thirty-five gateways that gave access to the city remain, but references to them have been preserved in such placenames as Plaza de Puerta Cerada (Closed Gate Square) and Plaza de Puerta de Moros (Moors Gate Square).

SYMBOLISM OF THE BLACK VIRGIN OF ALMUDENA

9

Calle de Bailén, 8–10
• Metro: Opera

> *Almudena: a fertility symbol*

The Black Virgin of the cathedral of Santa María la Real de la Almudena is a reproduction of the original statue that was lost in the Santa María church fire during the reign of Philip II. The current statue dates from the late sixteenth century, although it is believed that the head and hands of the Virgin, as well as the head of baby Jesus, may have belonged to the original statue.

Legend says that the statue of the Virgin was brought to Madrid in AD 38 by St Calocero, one of the twelve disciples of the apostle St James the Greater (Santiago el Major). Many years later, in 712, when the army of the Visigothic King Roderick was routed during the Battle of Guadalete and the Arabs, under the command of Tariq and Moussa, took the small city of Madrid, the Christian inhabitants of the city hid the statue of the Virgin in a cavity of the *almudena*, which is Spanish for "citadel". With time, the Christians forgot about this hiding spot, until the day when the Virgin appeared before the Cid to ask him to retake Madrid. In 1085, when the troops advanced towards the citadel, a portion of the wall fell away to reveal the miraculous Virgin, and it is at that very spot that the army entered and retook the city. Afterwards, King Alfonso VI of Castile ordered the sculpture of the Virgin to be placed on the altar of Santa María de la Almudena church, thus transforming this mosque into a church. From the twelfth to the early fourteenth centuries, the Templers worshipped the Virgin here, which, in a way, contributed to the renown of the city's patron saint.

During the Moorish domination, worship of the Virgin continued to be respected, as the Moors also venerated the Mother of God, in the person of Fatima, the fifth daughter of the Prophet Muhammad. They also respected Mary as the mother of the Prophet Isa, or Jesus. Thus, some authors interpret the word *almudena* as a synonym of the Virgin: "al", which means *alma* (Hebrew for virgin); "mu", which means woman; "dei" or God; "na" or *natus*, meaning born. The word thus stands for: virgin and woman or Mother of God.

The Black Virgin is also a symbol of fertility in farming villages. In this sense, the word *almudena* could be a derivative of the Arab word *almudín*, meaning "deposit of wheat", which referred to the wheat fields that surrounded the city and fed its inhabitants.

The fact that this Virgin was kept hidden for so long meant that she was a black occult goddess, which is symbolised by the moon found at her feet, as the moon is the mother of creation whose phases determine the sowing and harvesting seasons.

BLACK VIRGINS: VESTIGES OF PRE-CHRISTIAN RELIGIONS?

The Black Virgins are effigies of the Virgin Mary (sculptures, icons, paintings) which, for the most part, were created between the eleventh and fourteenth centuries. Their name refers quite simply to their dark colour.

Around 500 of them have been counted, mainly around the Mediterranean basin. Usually found in churches, some of them have been the object of major pilgrimages.

According to the Roman Catholic Church, there is no theological basis for the colour of these Virgins, although some experts have pointed to the passage in the Song of Songs (1:5): "*Nigra sum sed formosa*" which can be translated as "I am black but beautiful".

Some other very simple reasons have been proposed to explain this black colouring: the colour of the material used (ebony, mahogany, or a dark local wood) or deposits of soot from votive candles. But the importance that this colour has taken over time (some images have even been repainted black during restorations) leads to the belief that a deeper force is at work.

Thus, for some, the colour of the Black Virgin is a reminder that the Virgin, like the Catholic religion in general, did not become established *ex nihilo*, but replaced other ancient faiths in Western Europe: the Mithraic cult (for more details on this fascinating cult which was fundamental in creating a European identity, see *Secret Rome* in this series of guides), Mother-goddess cults, the cult of the Egyptian goddess Isis bearing Horus in her arms, etc.

In these archaic contexts, tribute was often rendered to the Mother goddess, symbol of fertility, gestation, procreation, regeneration, and renewal of life in general, on which the peasantry relied to ensure a bountiful harvest.

As the Christian religion began to affirm itself, the Virgin, mother of Jesus, son of God the Creator, thus became associated with this Mother goddess.

In symbolic terms, the black colour of the Virgin naturally evokes that of the virgin earth as well as the maternal/regenerative side of life in the sense that feminine procreation takes place in the (dark/black) depths of the woman's uterus. And her dark colour may also have brought her closer to the peasants whose own skin darkened from working out in the fields in the sun.

So it is therefore no accident if similar inscriptions are found on certain statues of Isis as on many of the Black Virgins: "*Virgini parituræ*" (to the Virgin who will give birth).

Finally, although many of the Black Virgins are associated with miracles, it is interesting to note that these events are usually linked to the beginning of a new cycle or a new era, thus respecting the image of the Virgin as the giver of life, above all else.

NATIONAL BROTHERHOOD OF VETERAN LEGIONNAIRE KNIGHTS

San Nicolás, 11
- Open Monday–Friday from 10am to 8pm
- Tel: 91 541 43 58
- Metro: Opera

> *Discovering the world of the legionnaires*

Today, in the former halberdier barracks, which became the barracks of the Guardia de Asalto (assault unit: a special police guard during the Second Republic), and then those of dictator Franco's guard, you can see the emblem of the Legion, not to mention a legionnaire, marking the entrance to the little-known Hermandad de los Antiguos Caballeros Legionarios (Brotherhood of the Veteran Legionnaire Knights) of Madrid. Theoretically, only legionnaires, members and sympathisers are admitted, but, except on rare occasions, curious visitors are also allowed in. To the sound of a military march playing in the background, you go into what appears to be a typical pub, even though numerous objects, ensigns, flags, photographs and posters testify to the Legion's evolution and heroic moments. With the permission of the pub owner, you can even visit the meeting room, the office of the President of the brotherhood, and the small library.

Another point of interest of this place is the price of a meal: €7. On the way out you can do a bit of shopping and offer yourself a book of military history, a keychain, a lighter or a pen bearing the legion's emblem.

UNBUTTONED SHIRT AND GOAT MASCOTS

People have always been intrigued by the appearance of the legionnaires due to their lack of formality. Their unbuttoned shirt, which reveals the chest, nevertheless evokes the virility and the power of the legionnaires.

The goat, the mascot of the legionnaires, symbolises the fact that, no matter how steep the slope, nothing will keep a legionnaire from reaching the top.

The Legion, also called the Tercio de Extranjeros (Battalion of Foreigners), owes its existence to Commander José Millán Astray, who understood the need to create a military regiment similar to the French Foreign Legion. Millán was injured several times and lost an eye and an arm in battle. His personal life was marked by his marriage to a woman who, on the day after their marriage, revealed that she had made a vow of eternal chastity. He was also quite fond of Japanese poetry.

SCULPTURE OF *ACCIDENTE AEREO*

Calle de los Milaneses, 3
• Metro: Ópera

And an angel falls from the sky ...

The sculpture on the terrace of No. 3 Calle de los Milaneses has given rise to much speculation. This upside-down figure, its wings twisted and mangled, has been seen in relation to the monument to the Fallen Angel in Buen Retiro gardens (and considered by many to be one of the world's rare public gestures of homage to Lucifer). Unconvincingly, it has also been argued that this sculpture is that of Icarus, who burnt his wings by flying too close to the Sun. Over time, the curiosity of the local residents has become that of casual strollers and tourists, who stop in Calle Mayor to look upwards and observe this incongruous angel, not only crushed in defeat but also about to tumble from the cornice.

The sculpture is the work of the artist Miguel Ángel Ruiz. In 2005 the owners of the apartment on the top floor (friends and clients of the artist) asked Ruiz to create a bronze sculpture with a copper-finish patina. The work is actually entitled *Accidente aereo* ("Aerial Accident") and the figure is inspired by neither Lucifer nor Icarus. The artist describes him as a man who, having set off for a stroll some 10,000 years ago, now returns, flying on his back so that he can play with the clouds. In this position, however, the man does not notice that cities have been built during his absence, occupying the space which he remembers as open fields.

NEARBY

HISTORY OF PLAZA MAYOR ENGRAVED ON FOUR BENCHES

Given that the benches in Plaza Mayor are almost always occupied, it is difficult to see the illustrations that were engraved upon them in the 1980s. These recount the adventures of this city square during its six centuries of existence. There are, for example, depictions of the three great fires of 1631, 1670 and 1790; the Carnival and masked balls that used to be held here; the *auto-da-fés* during which heretics were burned at the time of the Inquisition. But as well as such tragic and bloody episodes as public executions, the engravings also record the corridas and theatrical performances that were staged here for public entertainment.

CALLE MAYOR, 61

• Metro: Sol, Ópera

> **Smallest building in Madrid**

With a frontage of just 5 metres, the building at No. 61 Calle Mayor is considered the narrowest in the city. Right up to his death on 25 May 1681, this place was home to the eminent Spanish poet and playwright Pedro Calderón de la Barca, author of such works as *La vida es sueño* (*Life is a Dream*).

The building was saved from destruction thanks to the vehement opposition of Don Ramón de Mesonero Romanos, the official chronicler of late nineteenth-century Madrid. He actually took his stick to the workmen about to begin demolition work. Ultimately, the City Council agreed with the renowned chronicler and recognised the historical importance of the building.

For a long time the title of "smallest building in the city" was, however, held by the Casa de las cinco tejas (House of the five tiles) in Calle Santa Ana, which actually had only five tiles on its tiny roof. Unfortunately, that house was destroyed in 1851.

Nearby, at No. 6 Calle Postas, is another very narrow house. On the ground floor is an old shop selling religious vestments which is mentioned by the popular writer Benito Pérez Galdós in his *Fortunata y Jacinta*.

SHORTEST STREET

Calle Rompelanzas (Shaftbreaker Street), between Calle Carmen and Calle Preciados, is the shortest street in the city.

It was created by demolishing a few ruined buildings and thus opening up another approach to the church of Carmen Calzado. In the later sixteenth century Calle Rompelanzas was even narrower than it is now, so much so that the first carriage that tried to negotiate it ended up with a broken shaft.

That carriage actually belonged to the magistrate who had ordered the demolition of the houses, Luis Gaítán de Ayala. It was this incident that gave the street its name.

PASTRIES OF JERÓNIMAS DEL CORPUS CHRISTI CONVENT

Plaza del Conde de Miranda, 3
• Open Monday–Friday from 9.30am to 1pm and 4pm to 6.30pm
• Metro: Ópera, Sol

"Ave Maria"

I n Plaza del Conde de Miranda, an inconspicuous door marks the entry to the Corpus Christi convent. After ringing and hearing the "Ave Maria", you enter a place of solitude and silence, where an arrow directs you to the tower that allows the cloistered nuns a limited contact with the outside world.

Here you can buy the nuns' pastries: *rosquillas* (small ring-shaped cakes), almond and aniseed biscuits (particularly good), and *naranjines* (orange sweets). They are sold through a revolving door that allows the nuns to remain unseen. A pound costs €7.50 and a kilo €15.

The convent is known as the Convento de las Carboneras (Convent of the Coal Cellars), because a painting of the Immaculate Conception was discovered in a coal cellar and given to the nuns by a Franciscan friar. It was founded with the authorisation of King Philip III, by Doña Beatriz Ramírez de Mendoza, the Countess of Castellar, on a property belonging to her family. Doña Beatriz, a lady-in-waiting of Anne of Austria (queen consort of King Louis XIII of France), was a rather controversial figure. She founded three convents of the Mercedarian Order, but was expelled from one of them by the Superior-General of the Order due to her intrigues at court. The building, the work of the architect Miguel de Soria, has remained practically intact since its foundation.

NEARBY

SECRET GARDEN AT NO. 7 CALLE SACRAMENTO

The Huerto de las Monjas (Nun's Kitchen Garden) is an unexpected haven of peace whose presence is by no means obvious. To find it, you need to descend some steps and enter what seems to be the inner courtyard of a private house. But it is in fact a municipal garden open to the public.

This small hidden space once belonged to a Bernardine convent built in the seventeenth century and demolished in the 1970s to make room for a residential building. The nuns used to grow their vegetables here, but now you can rest in the shade of its old trees.

PAINTING ENTITLED *MATRITUM URBS REGIA*

Sobrino de Botín restaurant
Calle de los Cuchilleros, 17
• Open daily from 1pm to 6pm and 8pm to midnight
• Metro: Tirso de Molina, La Latina

An imaginary medieval Madrid

Considered to be the oldest restaurant in the world, *Sobrino de Botín* has in its first-floor rooms an enigmatic painting by the Russian artist Pierre Schild. Painted in 1956 and entitled *Matritum Urbs Regia,* the work aims to reproduce the appearance of Madrid in 1561 – a key date, when the city became the first permanent capital of the Spanish monarchy. Given that there are very few written records describing sixteenth-century Madrid, Schild based his work on drawings by Anton van den Wyngaerde, a Flemish landscape artist who from 1561 onwards travelled throughout Spain at the behest of Philip II and produced some sixty-two very detailed drawings of the various cities in the realm. His drawing of the new capital is considered to be the first panoramic view of Madrid and the most faithful surviving account of the urban fabric of the day.

As well as being a painter, Schild also worked as the art director on various films, including Buñuel's *Un chien andalou*. He was a special effects genius, introducing Spanish cinema to the "matte shot", a technique involving superimposed images. It was perhaps this aspect of his work which led him to imagine medieval Madrid in this way: while his image may contain a faithful reproduction of most of the buildings of the day, he does omit some and completely invent others.

Various features of the painting have been copied from elsewhere. The very title – *Matritum Urbs Regia* – was taken from Luis Texeira's map of the city, which may not have been the first to be drawn of Madrid but was certainly the most important and the most accurate.

A curious detail in Schild's painting is its inclusion of scaffolding. For example, this is to be seen on the right of the picture, corresponding to the location of the Torre Dorada, which was constructed between 1562 and 1569. The painting also shows the building of the stables (*las caballerizas*).

Among the structures that have been omitted are the churches of San Nicolás and San Pedro, which did already exist at this period. And certain buildings appear smaller than they actually were – for example, the Torre de los Lujanes – whereas others are not in exactly the right place.

The painting was part of an exhibition organised by the City Council in 1960. It was then forgotten about until the González family, the current owners of the restaurant, brought it back from obscurity to hang near the kitchen ovens where, for more than 300 years, this restaurant has prepared its famous wood-roast suckling pig.

CASAS A LA MALICIA

Calle del Toro and Calle Conde

> **Houses altered to deny the king's servants hospitality**

Calle del Toro and Calle Conde are like a number of streets in Madrid in that they contain houses which attract attention because of idiosyncratic differences in the size and positioning of windows. Known as *casas a la malicia* (spite houses), these date from the sixteenth century, when the royal capital was transferred from Toledo to Madrid. At the time Madrid did not have enough inns to meet its new role, for the transfer of the capital meant the arrival of not only the king but also his entire court and all those who hoped to make their fortune by being at the centre of power. There simply weren't enough rooms for everyone.

When the royal court had been itinerant, *regalia de aposento* (right of accommodation) had applied, requiring local residents to temporarily cede part of their own homes. However, when the court settled in Madrid, things changed: Philip II – himself housed in an *alcazar* that had been refurbished to his taste – ordered that the second floor of all houses should be made available for his servants, courtiers and state officials.

The new regulation sharpened the Madrilene ability to get by – that is, to turn things to their advantage. A number of residents undertook special building work, altering their houses in such a way that, from the outside, it was impossible to determine whether they had a second floor. A number of houses were built which apparently had only one floor but actually contained intermediate levels; and other houses suddenly sprouted attics or basements. Anything went when it came to avoiding the obligation to house the king's servants.

Up to 1,000 such *cases a la malicia* have been identified in Madrid. However, their deviousness often proved pointless: the houses that refused to lodge the king's servants had to pay a fine.

The transfer of the capital also created other logistical problems: food supplies, the need to widen streets and demolish old defences, the shortage of churches and hospitals. Furthermore, essential services such as sewers and drains had to be provided, and buildings erected to house public institutions. From being a city of barely 75 hectares, Madrid had to be transformed into a capital worthy of the realm: the scale of the change is indicated by the fact that the city's population in 1561 (the year of the transfer) was between 10,000 and 20,000 but by the end of that century had grown to almost 100,000.

Other *casas a la malicia* can be seen in Calle Redondilla, Calle de Rollo and Calle de Pez. There are models of such houses in the Museo de la Ciudad (City Museum) at No. 140, Calle Principe de Vergara.

STATUE OF CRISTO DE LAS LLUVIAS ⓲

San Pedro el Viejo church
Calle del Nuncio, 14
• Metro: La Latina

> **Reminder of a miraculous bell of San Pedro el Viejo Tower**

The Mudejar tower of San Pedro el Viejo church is the setting of an unusual legend surrounding the large bell that appeared at the top of the tower without anyone knowing how it got there. To try to explain this incident that took place in the sixteenth century, the local residents invented a strange story which told how the workers tried to pull the clock up to the top of the tower, but to no avail; so they decided to go home. Yet the next morning, everyone could hear the bell ring but no one could explain how it had got there, or who had completed the job.

Traditionally, the bell was rung to keep away the rain or, on the contrary, to beseech rain to fall. But the locals were alarmed each time they heard it ring because of the deafening sound it made. This continued until 1565, when the bell cracked, to the great relief of the residents of Madrid. It was finally removed and replaced in 1801 by a much smaller bell.

But the tradition surrounding the great bell hasn't disappeared: it is kept alive by the evocation of the Cristo de las Lluvias (Christ of the Rains), whose statue can be found in the church. It is said that the statue has the power to make it rain in times of drought and to calm tempests and storms.

The impressive sculpture is generally taken on procession on Holy Thursday. Depending on your point of view, it can be interpreted in two different ways: a proud Muslim caliph or a solemnly sorrowful Christ.

On the tower, you'll also find various royal coats of arms, one of which predates the period of the Catholic kings, Ferdinand II of Aragon and Isabella I of Castile (fifteenth century).

The church is named "San Pedro el Viejo" (Saint Peter the Elder) because it is one of the oldest parishes in Madrid: first mention of it can be found in a charter dated 1202 about an ancient Mozarabic construction on Puerta Cerrada square. In the fourteenth century, King Alfonso XI may have had the church built over the former Arab mosque, using the minaret to create the Mudejar tower, in memory of the victory against the Moors in the Battle of Algeciras. In the seventeenth century, the church was renovated in the style of the period. Some features of the medieval edifice were left untouched, however, such as the tower and the central nave, with its fifteenth-century Gothic choir. The church was originally called San Pedro el Real, but it lost this appellation in 1891.

A MOORISH TOWER THAT SERVED AS AN ASTRONOMICAL OBSERVATORY
This beautiful and slender Moorish brick tower reveals a line of denticulated motifs through the openings of the bell tower and, below, a curious yet pretty Arab-Byzantine window. Two motives encouraged the ancient builder monks to carry out this construction. First of all, it was meant to serve as a watchtower so that nearby residents could be warned and brought together if the enemy approached and, secondly, it was to serve as an astronomical observatory.

MUSEUM OF SAN ISIDRO COLLEGE

Calle Toledo, 39
- Tel: 91 365 1271
- Visits: only on Thursdays at 6pm
- Admission free but telephone booking required

> *A real cabinet of curiosities*

Founded by Jesuits, San Isidro College is the oldest educational establishment in Madrid: teaching has continued uninterrupted here since 1566, the one exception being during the Civil War when the building served as an air raid shelter. Students have included monarchs, great writers and Nobel prizewinners, and their school records are carefully preserved in a small museum in the cloister area.

The place is a real wonder: with limited means and a collection that is not very extensive, the teachers and students involved in the project have produced an accurate reflection of the world of education in the early twentieth century. The material in the display cases gives a vivid idea of a period when education relied on visual images, books and the sort of anatomical models that now strike us as very old-fashioned – indeed, as collectors' items.

A wide period staircase in stone and wood links the five floors, where display cases contain a variety of surprising objects. For example, there are various stuffed animals, some of them now threatened with extinction (such as the capercaillie). There are also such veterinary curiosities as stuffed "Siamese twin" goats.

The most astonishing exhibits are perhaps the veterinary models that can be taken apart and reassembled. These were intended to explain the internal workings of animals and let students identify the different parts of such creatures as a viper or a snail.

The real gem of the whole collection, however, is a wooden skeleton dating from the late nineteenth century; it too can be fully dismantled and reassembled.

If the guide has time, the tour might finish by passing through the monks' crypt, the burial ground of those who died during the religious persecutions of 1936.

CAPILLA DEL OBISPO

Plaza de la Paja, 9
• Open Tuesdays, Wednesdays and Thursdays 1pm to 2pm. Monday-Friday 6.30pm to 7.30pm. Saturdays and Sundays 12.30pm to 1.30pm
• Metro: La Latina

A small Gothic gem

The Capilla del Obispo (Bishop's Chapel) is a veritable gem of Gothic art that has survived over the centuries. Now, after three years of restoration work and an investment of 2 million euros, visitors can finally view this small oratory, which forms part of the church of San Andrés and the chapel of San Isidro.

The history of the chapel is closely linked with the life of San Isidro, the patron saint of Madrid, and with the Vargas family, one of the most powerful in the city and Isidro's employers. It was this family which commissioned the building of the chapel in 1520, to act as the final resting-place for the saint. However, a few years later it was the church of San Andrés which took over custody of the saint's remains and the chapel became the personal crypt of the Vargas: to either side of the presbytery the tombs of Francisco de Vargas and Inés de Carvajal can still be seen.

The bishop referred to in the chapel's name is Guiterre de Carvajal, bishop of Plasencia and a member of the Vargas family. He supervised work here and commissioned the Valladolid-born sculptor Francisco Giralte to produce the magnificent retable in painted wood and the alabaster cenotaphs.

Plaza della Paja (Hay Square) owes its name to an ancient Christian custom: the local residents used to give the priests of the parish churches hay with which to feed their mules.

COAT OF ARMS OF CASA DEL PASTOR

Calle Segovia, 21
• Metro: La Latina

> ***The oldest coat of arms of Madrid***

The reconstruction of an even older coat of arms from the sixteenth century, the oldest coat of arms of Madrid, in granite, dates from the seventeenth century and graces the façade of the former Casa del Pastor (Shepherd's House). You can clearly make out the bear, the strawberry tree, and the seven stars of the constellation Ursa Major that constitute the emblem of the city of Madrid. A small part of the arms was damaged in 2007: for some inexplicable reason holes were drilled into it to install a streetlamp, which was later removed.

For many years, Casa del Pastor was the seat of the municipal government for both Madrid and Toledo, and it was there that the first meeting of the City Council took place. The house was inhabited until the 1950s and demolished in 1972, despite the efforts of a coordinating body to defend the building as part of the city's heritage and restore it for tour visits. In 1988, the architect Francisco de Asís Cabrero y Torres-Quevedo constructed a new building on the site, and the old coat of arms was placed on the façade.

Beneath the house, there were four underground tunnels whose existence dates back to the Moorish period. Today they are sealed off, but they once allowed passage under much of the city: one tunnel ran towards the Manzanares river, another to the Royal Place, a third to the Almudena hill, and the fourth to Plaza de los Carros. But the exact routes of these subterranean galleries – which might have been converted into a tourist attraction like those of Paris or Rome – remains unclear.

LEGEND OF CASA DEL PASTOR

Casa del Pastor derives its name from the legend according to which the house once belonged to a priest named Don José who cared for the sick in his neighbourhood until he became infected with the plague. Before dying, he left his will in a sealed envelope: in it he bequeathed his house to the first person who entered the city by way of Puerta de la Vega on the morning of his death. And the first to pass through this city gate on the fateful day turned out to be a shepherd with his flock of sheep. Curiously, the legend tells that, several years previously, this same shepherd offered refuge to the priest when he was forced to flee from the city following a run-in with the Inquisition.

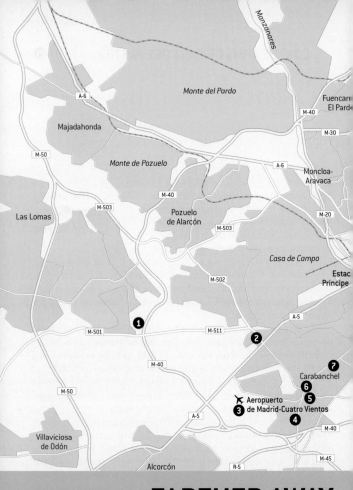

FARTHER AWAY

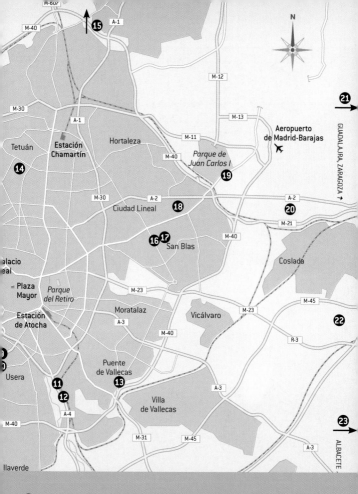

COMPUTER SCIENCE MUSEUM

Faculty of Computer Sciences, Technical University of Madrid
Building 5 (Reading Room)
• Open Friday from 12.30pm to 1.30pm and 3.30pm to 4.30pm
• Guided tours: 91 336 66 07
• Admission free
• Bus 571 from Moncloa

> *Computers with less memory capacity than a modern cell-phone*

T he Computer Science Museum brings together a wide range of computers which until recently were seen as being at the cutting edge of technology but which now seem a distant memory. This pantheon of obsolete material, vestiges of a recent past, is a telling measure of the incredible speed at which time moves forward when it comes to technological developments.

One of the museum's oldest exhibits is Spain's only extant ferrite memory. It was made in 1950, predating the arrival of integrated circuits, and was one of the first information storage systems.

The most popular exhibits are personal computers such as the Apple II Europlus (1979), or the Sinclair ZX Spectrum from IBM, which comes closest to resembling today's laptop except that it weighs over 10 kilos … Among the more recent models on display are the Commodore 64, the Toshiba T1000SE and the Apple Macintosh Plus, while among the bulkiest is the Secoinsa 40 (1975), weighing in at over 800 kilos. All these computers are in perfect working order even though they are totally useless by today's standards, as they have less memory capacity than a simple cell-phone.

ADA, COUNTESS OF LOVELACE, DAUGHTER OF LORD BYRON: THE FIRST COMPUTER PROGRAMMER

Incidental to the 1,500 or so exhibits in the museum are the often surprising anecdotes surrounding those who dedicated their lives to the development of information technology. Augusta Ada Byron (1815–1852), better known as Lady Lovelace, was the daughter of the poet Lord Byron and, intriguingly, the first computer programmer in history and a pioneer of computerised calculation. As a child, she was separated from her father because her mother was terrified by the idea that her daughter might develop the same artistic gifts as Byron. Lady Lovelace went on to devote her life to mathematics and created a number of programs to resolve complex calculations. The ADA computer programming language was named in her honour.

MUSEO Y ARCHIVO DEL CUERPO DE VETERINARIA MILITAR

2

Darío Gazapo, 3
• Tel: 91 512 25 00
• Open Monday to Friday from 10am to 1pm
• Metro: Colonia Jardín
• Bus 65
• Access on request only

L ocated in the Centro Militar de Veterinaria de la Defensa, the interesting and little-known Military Veterinary Museum can only be visited on request.

Collection of orthopaedic horseshoes

You will find items illustrating the evolution of veterinary medicine over the last fifty years. Notably there is a forge and bellows that were taken into war zones to shoe horses, as well as a collection of orthopaedic horseshoes.

The "souvenir room" of the museum showcases a large collection of surgical instruments, such as lancets, scalpels, dissection tweezers and hammers. You can also see extremely original models illustrating former methods of worming, operating or generally taking care of horses, as well as a special saddle adapted to carry a wounded soldier's stretcher.

The room is not very large but has several sections describing the various functions of the Centro Militar de Veterinaria since it was set up in 1942. There are also a range of uniforms, medical kits for cattle, statutory equipment for an army in the field and a collection of 130 flacons for various preparations. Although this museum is open to all, it is most used by vets.

AIR SHOWS BY THE FUNDACIÓN INFANTE DE ORLEÁNS   ❸

Cuatro Vientos aerodrome
• Tel: 91 321 18 57
• Aeronautical Museum open Tuesday–Saturday from 11am to 2pm
Air shows: first Sunday of the month (except January and August) at
11am
• Admission: €5

> *1930s planes in the Madrid skies*

O n the first Sunday of the month at Cuatro Vientos aerodrome, the Fundación Infante de Orleáns, which is dedicated to the preservation of vintage aircraft in Spain, organises an air show unique in Madrid, where you can see 1930s aircraft fly by.

Aviation enthusiasts or the plain curious will have an unforgettable experience seeing such aircraft taking off, as the Polikarpov I-16, a Soviet plane that played an important role in the Spanish Civil War.

The fabulous collection of twenty-three planes and seventeen different models notably includes a light transport plane, the British Aircraft Swallow, a Bücker Bü 131 (used by the Luftwaffe in the Second World War), a Piper J-3 (short take-off and landing), and a Cessna O-1 Bird Dog (built specially for the United States military in the 1950s), although the aerobatics carried out by the Sukhoi Su-26 are one of the high points of the show.

You can view the planes from Tuesday to Saturday in the museum, but nothing beats the pleasure of seeing them fly.

The monthly show begins at 11am, although you can wander around the planes beforehand where they are parked up by the runway. An aeronautic expert spells out the history and technical specifications of each plane. An hour later, the pilots climb aboard and take the planes up, weather permitting.

FLY IN A HISTORIC PLANE

The Fundación Infante de Orleáns owes its name to the military aviator Alfonso de Orleáns. Personal memorabilia, such as his uniform and flying goggles, are also on display in the museum.

The foundation, established in 1989, is dedicated to the research, restoration and promotion of the Spanish historic aeronautical heritage. To join, you need to complete a form and pay a subscription of 60 per year. One of the most sought-after members' privileges before the air show is to take part in a lottery for a seat during a flight. The lucky winner flies as a passenger in a Dornier 27.

BAMBOO CUBE

Los Clarinetes, 13
• Metro: Carabanchel Alto

A bamboo building

I n the Ensanche de Vallecas district, don't miss the ecological building that looks like a vast oriental cabin: its special feature is simply that it is made from bamboo.

Constructed by the Foreign Office Architects (FOA) firm run by Alejandro Zaera y Farshid Moussavi, for the "Empresa Municipal de la Vivienda", the building comprises eighty-eight apartments subsidised to make them affordable to young people up to 35 years who are low wage earners and would otherwise remain at home with their parents, as frequently happens in Spain.

Although from a distance you only see a simple windowless bamboo cube, as you draw nearer you notice adjustable double windows. The small apartments are comfortable and even enjoy a 1.5 metre terrace on the east and west façades, and 0.5 metre balconies to the north and south. All the apartments benefit from their dual aspect, allowing the air to circulate, which is particularly appreciated in the torrid summer heat of Madrid. Both inside and outside, natural materials have been chosen: the car park, for example, is covered with greenery. The building itself takes up less than half of the grounds, the rest of which are given over to gardens and games areas. Finally, so that the façade is not spoiled with graffiti, a metal enclosure protects the basement.

The bamboo used for this project, a particularly quick-growing variety called *Guadua angustifolia*, is found in many countries of Asia and the tropics, from Mexico to southern Argentina. It is widely used in these regions and was already a building material over 9,000 years ago.

COLONIA DE LA PRENSA

Rodríguez Lázaro, 1
• Metro: Eugenia de Montijo

*Architectural
avant-garde
of 1910*

In the Carabanchel district is an eye-catching arch supported by twin towers and a canopy. On the wrought-iron and ceramic canopy the following inscription can be read *"Colonia de la Prensa"* (Press Community). This modernist construction is the entrance to a district that spearheaded the urban development of Madrid at the beginning of the twentieth century.

Colonia de la Prensa was created because of the need to expand the city and develop the zone between Carabanchel Alto and Bajo. It was so named because it was inhabited by a group of journalists and writers known as *"Los Cincuenta"* (*"The Fifties"*).

Construction began on this first Spanish journalists' city in 1913 under the auspices of architect Felipe Mario López Blanco. The spacious plot, which had a great influence on contemporary design, was laid out with modernist housing. Only a few houses survive today: many of them were destroyed during the Civil War, and those untouched by war were demolished in the demand for real estate and the need to build upwards.

Until 1948, the year it was incorporated into Madrid, Carabanchel was a peaceful village in the suburbs of the capital, which is why the journalists' cooperative chose it as a restful place to stay. From the 1950s Carabanchel was transformed into a working-class district, with each development leaving less space for the original houses. In 1980 there was an attempt to save a few residences for their architectural and historic value, particularly in Época and Diario La Nación streets (named after newspaper titles). Along these streets you can appreciate the modernist features that made Colonia de la Prensa a site of the architectural avant-garde.

LIFE IN A CITY VILLAGE

La Plaza de Carabanchel is the centre of the old part of this district which was, until the middle of the last century, a village at some distance from the capital. Strolling around here is like travelling back to another age, especially if you go up calle Monseñor Óscar Romero as far as the hermitage of Nuestra Señora de la Antigua. This Romano-Mudejar style church dates from the thirteenth century, and first-century Roman remains have been found on the same site.

CALLE DE LEÓN V DE ARMENIA ❻

• Metro: Carpetana

> **Leo V,
> the king
> who made Madrid
> the capital
> of Armenia**

Not many residents of Madrid, passing by Calle de León V de Armenia near Via Carpetana, can claim to know the story of this extraordinary king who made Madrid the capital of Armenia.

Leo V or Levon V (sometimes referred to as Leon VI, 1342–1393), of the House of Lusignan, was the son of John of Lusignan and Soldane, daughter of George V of Georgia. Last sovereign of the Armenian Kingdom of Cilicia, he governed from 1374 to 1375. His reign was brief because his brother Constantine V attempted to kill him and he was forced to flee to Cyprus. Previously, he had been made a knight of the Order of the Sword in 1360 and appointed Seneschal of Jerusalem on 17 October 1372. In Cyprus, he married Marguerite of Soissons and the couple were crowned King and Queen of Armenia at Sis, according to both the Latin and Armenian rites. Following various battles against powerful Mamluk armies, he was imprisoned in the Cypriot castle of Kapan, and then transferred with his family to Cairo where he lived under the surveillance of the Egyptian sultan. His wife died during their captivity, sometime between 1379 and 1381.

The Franciscan monk Jean Dardel learned of Leon's plight while passing through Cairo on a pilgrimage to Jerusalem and persuaded King John I of Castile to intervene on his behalf. The Castilian monarch had to pay a sizeable ransom to the sultan to secure the release of Leon, who arrived ill and penniless at Medina del Campo in 1383. At this time, King John I, who was at Badajoz in western Spain to marry Princess Beatrice of Portugal, bestowed various honours and privileges upon the Armenian king and granted him the lordship of Madrid for life. Thus, Leon V of Armenia became Leon I of Madrid.

Leon governed Madrid justly and fairly, and was admired by all. He had the towers of the Royal Palace of the Alcazar rebuilt, allowed the municipal and royal functionaries to keep their posts, and even granted pardon in advance to those who disobeyed him. He was much loved in Madrid and throughout the Iberian Peninsula. The exiled king was also uncommonly tall: nearly 2 metres in height.

Following the death of his protector John I in 1390, Leon of Lusignan left Castile and went to France. He died in Paris in 1393, having tried in vain to reconcile the warring French and English courts in order to promote a new crusade that would allow him to recover his lands. He was buried at the convent of the Celestines in Paris, but his body was later moved to the Royal Basilica at Saint-Denis, where it still rests today.

MELUSINE THE FAIRY, FOUNDER OF THE HOUSE OF LUSIGNAN OF LEON V?

According to the legend propagated by French poet-composer Jean d'Arras between 1382 and 1394, Melusine, ancestor of Leon V, was the founder of the Lusignan lineage (the etymology of Melusine being "Mother of the Lusignans"): Elynas, King of Albany (a poetic name for Scotland, the "white land") met a very beautiful lady while out hunting in the woods one day.

She was Pressyne, mother of Melusine. The king wooed her and she agreed to marry him, but on one condition (as always in dealings between fairies and mortals, this proved fateful): the king was never to enter her chamber when she was giving birth or bathing her children.

Elynas agreed to this and married Pressyne, who gave birth to triplets.

But the king broke his word and Pressyne left him with her three daughters to go live on the lost isle of Avalon, sometimes associated with St Brendan's Island and the subterranean empire of Agharta.

The three daughters, Melusine, Melior and Palatyne, grew up in Avalon. When she was fifteen years old, Melusine, the most beautiful of the three, asked her mother why they had been taken to the island. When informed of her father's broken promise, she sought revenge. With her sisters, she locked Elynas inside a mountain.

But Pressyne was enraged by their disrespect and punished them. Melusine was condemned every Saturday to take the form of a serpent from the waist down. Afterwards, she was exiled to the enchanted forest of Poitou, near the Fountain of Thirst. It was there that the knight Raymond of Poitou, returning from a boar hunt, found her bathing in the moonlight, was smitten with love, and asked her to marry him. Just as her mother had done, she agreed on one condition: that he should never enter her chamber on Saturdays.

Raymond agreed but then broke his promise, and saw her bathing, half-woman, half-serpent. She forgave him, but fate was already set in motion. During a quarrel, he called her "serpent" in front of the court.

She then gave him two magic rings and, taking the shape of a winged dragon, she flew from a window with a cry of unspeakable pain, disappearing forever.

So according to legend, the fairy Melusine was the ancestor of Leon of Lusignan as well as of Madrid. It is also said that Leon had no difficulty in discovering the site of Raymond's tomb at the monastery of Montserrat, in Catalonia.

LUSIGNAN DYNASTY: KEEPERS OF THE HOLY GRAIL?

The reign of the Lusignan dynasty over the Armenian kingdom of Cilicia (Lesser Armenia) lasted from 1341 with Constantine IV until 1375 with Leon V.

This dynasty distinguished itself mainly by the Gnostic secrets said to be possessed by some of its members: with Guy of Lusignan (reigned 1150–1194), they were the first noble dynasty to occupy the throne of Jerusalem, considered to be the centre of the world by the Christians of the Middle Ages.

They were thus considered to be the "kings of the world".

According to spiritual tradition, it was also the Lusignans who took the Holy Grail from Jerusalem, first to Cyprus and then to Armenia.

The legend in which Melusine ("Mother of the Lusignans") was joined to Raymond (whose name means "king of the world") to create the dynasty thus gains its full sense in legitimising the Lusignans' position: the union of the fairy with Raymond symbolises the gift of divine knowledge to the

family, and more specifically, the Holy Grail entrusted to its care.

In the legend, the fact that Raymond may not look upon Melusine on Saturday (the Sabbath day in Hebraic tradition) is a reminder that this is the day on which God rested after Creation.

It is also a day of reflection, when physical activities are set aside in favour of spiritual exercises, during which divine grace is revealed to man, initiating him to secret knowledge about which he must maintain silence.

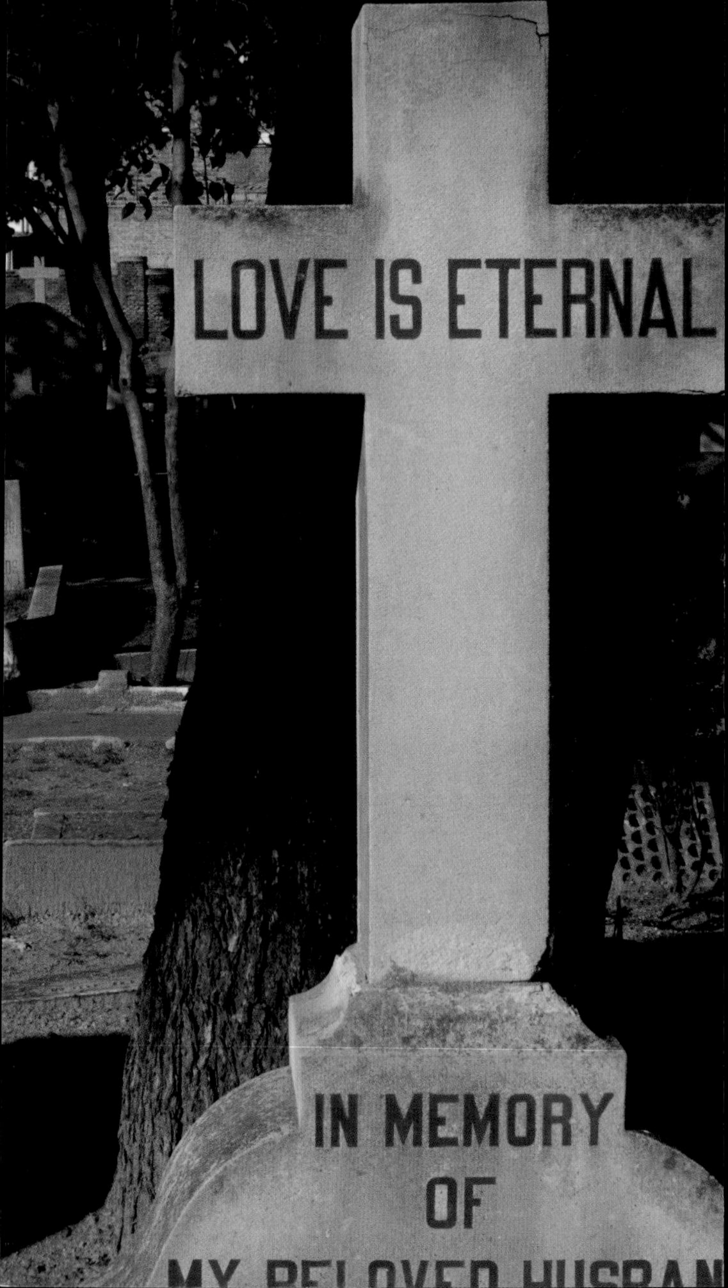
LOVE IS ETERNAL
IN MEMORY
OF

BRITISH CEMETERY

Calle Comandante Fontanes, 7
• Tel: British Consulate General 91 524 97 18
• Open Tuesday, Thursday and Saturday from 10.30am to 1pm
• Metro: Urgel

F ramed by calle de Irlanda and calle de Inglaterra in the Carabanchel district is one of the least-known places in Madrid, the first and only British cemetery in the city. It was inaugurated in 1854 to offer a burial ground for Protestants because they weren't accepted in any other cemetery. Although the cemetery was originally intended for British subjects, over time people from other faiths were buried there (Lutherans, member of the Greek and Russian Orthodox Church, Jews and even Muslims), as well as members of various cults. As Spanish law prohibited their burial in municipal cemeteries, the non-Catholic foreign communities chose this little plot in a typically English style for their final resting-place.

> *Piece of the United Kingdom at Carabanchel*

Among the mausoleums take note of the one belonging to the Parish family, originally from Stafford and the founders of Madrid's famous Price Circus, and that of Emilio Lhardy, the Swiss designer of the city's first elegant restaurant in 1839, a veritable institution which still retains its discreet ambience. The graves of the Austro-Hungarian banking family of Bauer are also here, and the Terstch funerary monument attracts attention with its Masonic symbols. Loewe, Girod and Boetticher are more famous names, not to mention the princes of the Bagration dynasty, originally from Georgia.

This tranquil place holds approximately 600 graves, and the tombstones evoke past histories of luxury, exile and espionage: among the incumbents of the cemetery are members of the British Secret Service.

Today almost no funerals take place here, but there is still space to bury ashes in the evocative landscape of a cemetery over 150 years old.

LAND BELONGING TO GREAT BRITAIN

The British coat of arms welcoming visitors on the brick façade is also indicative of a notable special feature: the plot enjoys the privileges of extraterritoriality, just like the embassies, and thus belongs to the UK Government.

SCULPTURE OF SANTA MARÍA DE LA CABEZA ⑧

Pont de Toledo
Glorieta de las Pirámides
• Metro: Marqués de Vadillo

The miraculous and forgotten widow of San Isidro

Strolling across the Pont de Toledo over the Manzanares river, you can see a stone niche protecting a forgotten sculpture of Santa María de la Cabeza, the widow of San Isidro (St Isidore), male patron saint of Madrid.

This bridge was built between 1718 and 1732 by the architect Pedro de Ribera, who was probably inspired by a legendary episode from the life of Santa María and San Isidro: each night, María dreamed that the mother of Christ could cross the Jarama river by spreading her cape on the waters. It was in memory of this event that the Toledo bridge was built.

Santa María de la Cabeza's original name was María Toribia. She was born in the twelfth century at Guadalajara and lived at Torrelaguna, in Madrid province, dying between 1175 and 1180. Throughout her life she proved herself to be devoted, pious, and greatly charitable. On several occasions she retreated from the world to live as a hermit, which gave rise to mistaken ideas about her life, with some saying that she was an uneducated peasant. This was later denied by the religious military order of the Templars. At the side of her husband Isidro, whom she met while he was fleeing from the Almoravid conquest, she underwent numerous religious studies and became an expert in the cult of the Virgin Mary, for whom the Templars showed great devotion. On her death, she was buried in the Visigothic church of Santa María which she had diligently attended, on the banks of the Jarama near Torrelaguna, a property that belonged to the Order of the Templars until 1311. There, her head was placed in a reliquary on the main altar of the oratory. After the disbanding of the Templars, the saint's body and head were transported to the Franciscan convent of Nuestra Señora de la Piedad de Torrelaguna and preserved in the sacristy in an ivory coffer. The relics remained there until they were again transferred, this time to Madrid, in 1645. Then in 1769 they were moved from the oratory of Casas Consistoriales to the altar of Collégiale de San Isidro, where the relics of her husband are venerated to this day.

All these details, examined by the apostolic authorities, led Pope Innocent XII to beatify her and confirm the immemorial cult of the servant of God on 11 August 1697. Thus the name of Santa María de la Cabeza was inscribed on the list of martyrs: her feast day is celebrated on 9 September.

The Middle Ages was not a male-dominated period. In the twelfth century, convent life was conducive to great intellectual energy, as shown by Hildegarde von Bilgen, a studious and mystic German nun, or again Juliana of Norwich, England.

Most of the women involved in the clergy were spouses helping out their husbands, or else widows leading a more independent life. Such was the case of Santa María de la Cabeza, widow of San Isidro and mother of San Illán, who embodied the very spirit of enlightened medieval women who knew how to unite faith and wisdom.

Symbolically, the saint's presence makes this bridge a passage between the human and the spiritual worlds which recalls the Latin term *pontifex* (bridge-builder). The Pope (pontiff) is literally an intermediary between two worlds.

MASONIC SCULPTURES OF THE PASILLO VERDE FERROVIARIO ❾

Place Ortega y Munilla
Corner of Calle del Ferrocarril and Paseo de las Delicias
Calle Santa María la Real de Nieva

> **The obelisk: a simplified version of the ancient Egyptian pyramids**

In the Arganzuela neighbourhood, three obelisks bear inscriptions alluding to Freemasonry. Two of them are identical (with triangular bases and pyramidal crowns) and stand in open spaces, near the modern railway stations of Delicias and Pirámides. The third obelisk, crowned by an inclined plane, is smaller and found in a quieter, less accessible spot.

These obelisks, the work of architect Manuel Ayllón, are located along the so-called Pasillo Verde Ferroviario (Green Railway Corridor) in Calle Santa María la Real de Nieva, Place Ortega, and at the corner of Calle del Ferrocarril and Paseo de las Delicias. The three monuments bear the inscription "*Lau-Deo*" ("God be Praised"), and represent the three principal Masonic virtues: Wisdom, Strength and Beauty.

The obelisk was an object of worship among the peoples of antiquity,

notably the Egyptians, who considered it to be their link with the Sun God whom they venerated under the name of *Per-Amen-Ra*. In Freemasonry, the obelisk represents the eternal Grand Orient and therefore the spiritual Sun.

The obelisk is also the refined form of the primitive Celtic menhirs and a simplified expression of the Egyptian pyramids. It acts as catalyst of celestial energy and as a capacitor of terrestrial energy, known by Orientals as *Fohat* and *Kundalini* and by Westerners as *sidereal tellurism* and *planetary tellurism*. The obelisk thus serves here as a central core that concentrates both types of energy, which it distributes to its surroundings and the beings within its zone of influence.

THE SOLOMONIC COLUMNS OF MADRID

In the same period when he created these obelisks, Manuel Ayllón also initially set up a series of columns marking the kilometres of the Green Railway Corridor, overlooking the passing trains. They were supposed to be made from green marble, but due to the high cost artificial stone was eventually used. All of them have now been destroyed by acts of vandalism, although some say they were removed for political reasons. Be that as it may, their remnants are now stored in municipal warehouses.

Placed at key points of the telluric forces that run through the city, the helical columns recall the two original bronze columns that stood at the entrance to the ancient Temple of Solomon in Jerusalem. Their Hebrew names *Jachin* and *Boaz* respectively mean "he will establish" and "the strength is in him". Taken together, this gives "By his strength, God will establish the temple and the religion of which He is the centre".

Traditionally, the *Jachin* column stood to the right of the Temple door and symbolised the Sun. Its colour was black or red. The *Boaz* column was on the left and symbolised the Moon. It was white or green. In the Hindu tradition, *Jachin* and *Boaz* are *Jnana* and *Bhakti*, or Wisdom and Love,

qualities that characterised the Great Enlightened Ones, known in the Orient as *Bhante-Jauls* (brothers in purity). They often bear the initials J.B. in their names, as for example John the Baptist, or Jesus, who was born and died in two places with the same initials: Bethlehem and Jerusalem.

In Madrid, the columns were judiciously placed near a railway line, where trains carried people from one destination to another, in constant transition, which is the ultimate significance of these Solomonic pillars.

SCULPTURES OF THE FIVE PLATONIC SOLIDS ❿

Plaza Ortega y Munilla: tetrahedron
Plaza Francisco Morano: hexahedron
Parc de las Peñuelas: icosahedron
Plaza de Santa Maria de la Cabeza: octahedron
Paseo de los Melancólicos (corner of Calle Santa Maria la Real de Nieva
and Calle Jemenuño): dodecahedron

Hermetism in Madrid

L ocated in different parts of the Arganzuela district, these five geometric forms (tetrahedron, hexahedron, icosahedron, octahedron and dodecahedron) are a great mystery due to the scarcity – indeed, absence – of information as to their symbolic meaning. The forms were created by the writer Luis Racionero and the architect Ismael Guarner, with another architect – Manuel Ayllòn – serving as advisor and initial driving-force behind the project. Their actual location is far from casual, as they mark points on the surface which correspond to the route of the new underground railway line.

The sculptures themselves depict the five Platonic solids that feature in the geometrical treatise written by Luca Pacioli (Sansepolcro, Italy, 1445–1517), a Franciscan friar who was a pioneer in the calculation of probabilities. In his most important work, *De divina proportione* ("About the Divine Proportions"), Pacioli deals with the issues raised by polygonal forms and discusses the rules of perspective that would play such a part in Quattrocento painting. He was also the teacher of Leonardo da Vinci.

The sculptures of the Platonic solids in Arganzuela may appear rather strange and incomprehensible to those who are used to urban decor taking a more figurative form. However, the works have a specific objective: to illustrate the perfections to be found in the world of nature and how the intelligence can transfer that perfection to the world of humankind.

Geometry is the discipline that is most clearly associated with Masonic initiation, and the architect Manuel Ayllòn sees the knowledge of numbers and their significance as a means of assessing progress up the scale of Masonic knowledge. The various levels that the apprentice must pass through before becoming a Master Mason are linked with the knowledge of geometry and its symbolic significance. 1 corresponds to unity, to the essence; 2 to the dialectic, to the male and the female; 3 to the Trinity, the sacred and divine; 4 to the four elements, and so on. In the case of the Platonic solids, each polyhedron is formed of elementary polygons whose two-dimensional form generates their three-dimensional occupation of corporeal space. The passage from 2 to 3 is an initiatory change by means of which the layman becomes one of the initiated, the apprentice becomes a Master Mason – a process which involves "leaving the shadows to find the light".

For further information on the relation between the five Platonic solids, the five natural elements (earth, air, water, fire and ether) and their respective planets, see the following double page.

THE FIVE BASIC SOLIDS AND SACRED GEOMETRY

Sacred geometry is a world vision according to which the basic criteria for existence are perceived as being *sacred*. Through them can be contemplated the *Magnum Misterium*, the Universal *Grand Project*, by learning its laws, principles and the inter-relationships of shapes. These universal shapes are systematised in a geometric complex in which each figure has its own mathematical and philosophical interpretation. They are applied in projects of *sacred architecture* and *sacred art*, which always use the "divine" proportions in which Man reflects the Universe, and vice versa. It is a common belief that *sacred geometry* and its mathematical relationships, which are harmonic and proportional, are also found in Music, Light and Cosmology. Man first discovered this system of values in prehistoric times, in the megalithic and Neolithic cultures, for example, and some consider it to be a universal facet of the human condition.

Sacred geometry is fundamental to the construction of sacred structures, such as synagogues, churches and mosques, and also plays a role in creating the interior sacred space of temples, through the altars and tabernacles. Passed down from Graeco-Egyptian culture and exported to ancient Rome, *sacred geometry* in the European Middle Ages inspired the creation of the Roman and Gothic architecture of Europe's medieval cathedrals, which incorporate this geometry of sacred symbolism.

It is said that Pythagoras (Samos, *c.* 570 BC – Metapontum, *c.* 497 BC) was the one who founded the system of *sacred geometry* in his school in

Croton, Greece. This Greek philosopher and mathematician is believed to have brought the knowledge he acquired in Egypt and India back to Greece. Using the golden ratio (1.618) and applying it to the geometric forms of the five basic solids, Pythagoras created the mathematical method universally known as *Pythagorean geometry*.

To create the five solids (the tetrahedron or pyramid, the hexahedron or cube, the octahedron, the dodecahedron and the icosahedron), about which Plato would later philosophise (to such a point that they would become known as the *five Platonic solids*), Pythagoras was inspired by the Greek myth about the child-god Dionysus' toys: a basket, dice, top, ball and mirror. On a cosmic level, the *basket* represents the Universe; the dice, the *five Platonic solids* symbolising the natural elements (ether, air, fire, water, earth); the *top* is the atom of matter; the *ball*, the Earth's globe; and, finally, the *mirror* reflects the work of the Supreme Geometrist (*Dionysus*), which itself is the universal manifestation of Life and Consciousness, of God towards Man and vice versa. Each of the five Platonic solids also represents a planetary energy that is connected by its form to a natural element. Thus, the *dodecahedron* is traditionally linked to Venus and ether, the natural quintessence, expressed by a temple's dome. The *octahedron*, linked to Saturn and the air, represents the transept's cross. The *tetrahedron*, linked to Mars and fire, is symbolised by the openings in the temple through which light gushes forth. The *icosahedron*, linked to the Moon and water, establishes the harmony of forms in the temple *design*, constructing the connecting lines between the altars and columns. Finally, the *hexahedron* (cube), fixes the Sun to its element, the earth, by determining the shape of the temple's foundation or floor.

The main purpose of *sacred geometry* is thus to create Universal Perfection through perfect mathematical forms and calculations, and, by using *sacred architecture*, to connect the Multiple to the Single in a space that is geometrically dedicated to this end.

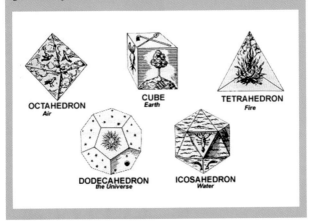

OCTAHEDRON
Air

CUBE
Earth

TETRAHEDRON
Fire

DODECAHEDRON
the Universe

ICOSAHEDRON
Water

Revista gráfica del m
Velocidad

CAMPEO

MUSEO ÁNGEL NIETO

Avenida del Planetario, 4; Parque Tierno Galván
• Tel: 91 468 02 24
• Open Tuesday–Friday from 11am to 6pm; Saturday and Sunday 10.30am to 2.30pm
• Admission: €1
• Metro: Méndez Álvaro

> **Memorabilia of a motorcycle champion**

Despite the Spanish passion for motorcycle racing, the small Ángel Nieto museum passes completely below the radar. Although it could be better maintained, it is still interesting simply because it pays tribute to a person still living.

Ángel Nieto is a hero: four times second in the world championships, ninety Grand Prix wins, twenty-three Spanish Championship titles on bikes of different capacities, and thirteen times World Champion, or "12+1", according to the extremely superstitious champion himself.

The museum retraces the story of this rider from Zamora, with emphasis on his great triumphs. You can admire all the bikes on which Nieto won the World Championship: machines that are now collectors' items and which in their day revolutionised the track, as for example the Minarelli 125cc, on which he won the 1979 Championship; the Sirocco 250cc, Spanish Championship in 1981, or the Garelli 125cc, thrice World Champion in 1982, 1983 and 1984.

Here you can also follow the evolution of competition bikes over the last thirty years, and the way in which they have been perfected: those from the

1960s have such a rudimentary chassis that you can't help wondering how they reached speeds of over 150 km/h.

The museum also showcases a vast quantity of objects that formed part of a champion's life at the time: his helmets, gloves and overalls. You can also look through contemporary press cuttings, the headlines and the magazines featuring Nieto. If you like, you can take away a souvenir poster signed by Nieto himself.

Today, Ángel Nieto has retired from active sport. He now works as a sports commentator and runs a Grand Prix motorcycle racing team with his son, Ángel Nieto Jr.

MASONIC SYMBOLS ON THE SOUTH GATE   ⑫
OF TIERNO GALVÁN PARK

• Metro: Méndez Álvaro

"ALGADU":
To the Great
Architect
of the Universe

Most of the people who stroll through Tierno Galván Park are probably unaware that the architectural and sculptural monument known as the Puerta del Sur (South Gate) displays numerous Masonic symbols. This monument was a project designed by the architect and town planner professor Manuel Ayllón, author of books such as *Conspiración contra el rey* ("The Plot Against the King") and *Golpe a Venecia* ("The Venetian Coup"), and advisor for the Green Railway Corridor (see p. 214). He also has a keen interest in Freemasonry.

At the top of the large metallic chimney of this park founded in honour of Enrique Tierno Galván (mayor of Madrid from 1979 to 1986), you can make out, if you have good eyesight or a pair of binoculars at hand, the letters ALGADU, an acronym for "Al Gran Arquitecto del Universo" (To the Great Architect of the Universe), a symbolic name used in Freemasonry to refer to the Creative Principle, independently of the religion practised by its members.

The access ramp (which represents the entry to Heaven) is painted in the classic colours, black and white, of Freemasonry. It is also important to note that the east-west axis is aligned with the astronomical positions of the rising and setting Sun. The north-south axis points northward to the Astronomical Observatory (the eye that lets you "read the heavens") and southward to Cerro Negro and Cerro de los Angeles, which constitute the true geographical centre of Spain, according to Manuel Ayllón.

On the floor of the South Gate, you can also see the typical chequered pattern that is associated in Masonic symbolism with the Square of Mercury, a symbol of the union of the liquid and the solid. The numbers 3 and 7, which have great significance in Masonic symbolism, are also present in the monument: there are three streetlamps on either side of the gate, 3 and 3 making reference to the number 33, the age of Christ when he was crucified, and the gate itself is 33 metres tall. The chimney has a height of 49 metres, 49 being the square of 7, which represents the entrance to Heaven.

> Architect Manuel Ayllón has also carried out other projects that include Masonic and esoteric elements in the same district of Madrid, such as the five Platonic solids found at various points in Arganzuela (see p. 217), and the three obelisks at Paseo de los Melancólicos, Plaza de Ortega y Munilla and the corner of Calle del Ferrocarril and Paseo de las Delicias (see p. 214).

OTHER MASONIC REFERENCES IN MADRID

The statue of Emilio Castelar (Plaza de Emilio Castelar), a work by the architect and Freemason Benlliure, is crowned by three allegories: Wisdom, Strength and Beauty, the great Masonic virtues.

Capilla de la Bolsa restaurant, once the site of the Madrid Stock Exchange, was also later a Masonic lodge.

Paseo de las Acacias. In Freemasonry, the acacia tree is linked to initiation and immortality. Many of the city mayors who were Freemasons planted acacias in the streets of Madrid, because they provided the preferred flowers of the Masonic orders.

Ministry of Agriculture (see p. 144).

MUSEO MUNICIPAL DE BOMBEROS

Calle de Boada, 4
- Open Monday–Friday from 10am to 1.30pm
- To book a visit: 91 478 65 72
- Metro: Portazgo

> *How Madrid's fire service began*

First opened in 1982, the Municipal Firefighters' Museum is housed in a hangar divided into several sections. In the documentation section, you can see photographs of the various incidents covered in the course of the nineteenth century as well as a collection of extinguishers, fire lances, transmission devices, radio telephones and insulated respiratory equipment from different eras.

The most attractive feature of the museum is however the collection of vehicles, some of which were so rudimentary that you can't help wondering how they could have been used in firefighting. Many of the water pumps were manual and the capacity of the tank in most vehicles wasn't enough to put out a fire.

The first great conflagrations of Madrid, which in a way brought the fire service into being, took hold at Puerta de Guadalajara and in the houses of Commander Pedro Zapata, near Plaza Mayor. Following these fires, the City Council signed the first fire agreement in mid 1577, which revealed the urgent need to get together a group of men qualified to help the population in case of fire. The first firemen were masons, carpenters and labourers, as it was thought their manual and physical skills would be useful in the work of firefighting. Thanks to this agreement, Madrid was equipped with fire sprinklers, leather buckets and ladders, among other equipment that was made available to these firemen.

In 1618, the mayor of Madrid, then Francisco de Villasis, decided that a group of twenty-four carpenters should devote themselves to "fighting against fires" in the city. The new delegates, known as *matafuegos* (fire soldiers) would receive payment for their work and had to be ready to rush to the fire whenever the church bells were rung in a certain way.

WHAT DOES THE INSCRIPTION "*ASEGURADORA DE INCENDIOS*" MEAN ?
This inscription, which can be read at the entrance to certain buildings, refers to a local residents' association founded in 1822 with the aim of mutual protection and indemnisation in case of fire in one of the buildings on the register. The association had a support group among the firemen, at the time rather casually organised.

MUSEO TIFLOLÓGICO RUN BY ONCE ⑭

Calle La Coruña, 18
- Tel: 91 589 42 19
- Open Monday–Friday from 11am to 2pm and 5pm to 8pm
- Metro: Estrecho

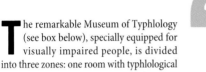

A touching museum

The remarkable Museum of Typhlology (see box below), specially equipped for visually impaired people, is divided into three zones: one room with typhlological material, another with works by blind or visually impaired artists, and a third presenting scale models of monuments from Spain and other countries.

The museum's exhibition space of 1,500 square metres on two floors is comprehensively laid out so that those with sight problems or wheelchair users can visit and interact with the displays.

The reproductions of famous monuments are perhaps the most surprising: the Roman Coliseum, the City of Jerusalem, the Gateway of the Sun at Tiahuanaco (Tiwanaku) in Bolivia and the Segovia aqueduct, among other monuments and sculptures that form part of world heritage, are all constructed from materials that let you appreciate the main features of their architecture by touching and feeling them.

The collection of typhlological material is also very interesting, as it brings together everything linked to culture and education from the mid nineteenth century that concerns teaching blind people writing, drawing, mathematics and music. You can learn the story of the development of Braille and other writing systems such as that of Llorens, Sor and Moon, who attempted to find

a writing formula valid for both blind and sighted people.

The exhibitions include a strange Braille-writing machine from the 1930s, several calculators adapted for the blind and a relief map of the Iberian peninsula dated 1879, the work of professor Francisco Just i Valentí (1842–1926), constructed from a variety of materials such as leather, paper, cardboard and differently textured fabric.

The word *typhlology* comes from the Greek *typhlós*, meaning blind.

BURR

BURROLANDIA

Autovia de Colmenar Viejo, Km. 21
(Tres Cantos-Soto de Viñuelas exit; check internet itinerary)
• Open Sunday from 11am to 1.30pm
• Tel: 630 058 428 / 639 962 728
• Admission free
• Ruta de Agua: adults, €8; children, €4
• www.amiburro.es
• Bus 716 from Plaza de Castilla

*Save
the donkeys!*

Burrolandia, just 15 minutes out of Madrid, is the only nature reserve within the Community of Madrid dedicated to the protection of donkeys. The reserve, maintained by the Asociación Amigos del Burro (Donkeys' Friends Association), is located in one of the region's most unspoilt areas, Soto de Viñuelas. The property, built by members of the association using recycled material, offers an experience of farming life in an environment shared with donkeys and other animals such as sheep, rabbits, chickens, pigs and even a bottle-fed deer. The main building is a sort of interactive agricultural museum, complete with various old ploughs and tools, which presents the biological life-cycle of the donkey within the context of ancestral working methods.

Burrolandia also offers a series of attractions, notably the Ruta del Agua (Water Route). This is a 3- to 4-hour excursion into the Viñuelas hills where children can alternate between walking, riding on docile little donkeys or taking one of the donkey-drawn carts. At the farm, they can also participate in different activities such as helping the shepherds shear the sheep or feeding and grooming the donkeys. There is even a painting workshop.

To raise money, the reserve sells cosmetic products made from asses' milk as well as a range of donkey-themed souvenirs (calendars, notebooks, T-shirts …); and it holds a small quarterly flea-market, although some items can be found on sale each Sunday. The principal aim remains the preservation of the donkey, whose population has been declining steadily, from 1 million in the 1970s to around 60,000 today. Burrolandia has not only saved abandoned or ill-treated animals, but has also seen the births of twenty-seven donkey foals and two "bardots" (cross between a male horse and a female donkey).

THE PROPERTIES OF ASSES' MILK

Asses' milk is the closest thing in nature to human mothers' milk. Its properties were already well known in ancient Egypt (Cleopatra is said to have bathed in asses' milk to preserve her beauty), as well as in Greece and Rome, and orphanages in Paris kept female donkeys to give their milk to children and to the sick. The milk contains fatty acids, retinol and vitamin B and has significant cosmetic, tissue-repairing and regenerative properties. Today, asses' milk is of less importance than in the past, not least because of its low yield (1 litre per day, compared with 20 litres for a cow) and because an ass only lactates from the age of 4.

FAUST SCULPTURE AT THE CEMENTERIO DE LA ALMUDENA

16

Avenida Daroca, 90
• Winter opening times: from 8am to 7pm (October–June)
• Summer: from 8am to 7.30pm (July–September)
• Tel: 91 510 84 64 / 91 510 84 69
• Metro: La Elipa
• Bus: 15, 28, 106, 110, 113, 210

> *The apocalyptic angel: myths and legends*

At the entrance to Almudena cemetery is a chapel whose cupola is crowned with an angel known to Madrilenes as Faust. The seated angel holds in his lap a trumpet which is the subject of a grim legend.

The statue really does have a very strange history linked to the inauguration of the cemetery dedicated to Nuestra Señora de la Almudena, patron saint of Madrid. This took place on 15 June 1884, a year before the planned date, because of the cholera that had swept through the city and led to the need for a temporary burial ground, the "epidemic cemetery".

Originally, the statue of Faust stood right at the entrance to the cemetery. But as it represented the angel announcing the Last Judgement, proclaiming with his trumpet the day when the dead would come to life, it terrorised the local people. So they promptly invented stories about the trumpet, some even swearing that they had seen a dead man walking among the sombre tombs while the instrument sounded. To hear it would mean that death was not far away …

The people's dread of this statue was so acute that it was moved and altered: thus, in 1924, (according to the most reliable sources), it was set on top of the modernist-style chapel built by architect García Nava in order to be less visible than before. One disturbing aspect of all this was that the original angel, sitting waiting for the Last Judgement, held the trumpet in his right hand at head height, whereas the new statue carries it in his lap. A means of warding off evil?

FAUST'S HIDDEN MESSAGE

Contrary to popular tradition which considers Faust to be the angel of death, the Latin word *Faustus* means *"happy, prosperous"*. Likewise, Judgement Day, far from signifying the end of the world, indicates "the end of", in the sense of the end of a cycle and the beginning of another: that of a new era in which humanity attains greater spirituality than before.

MASONIC SYMBOLISM IN CEMENTERIO DE NUESTRA SEÑORA DE LA ALMUDENA

17

Avenida Daroca, 90
• Winter opening times: from 8am to 7pm (October–June)
• Summer: from 8am to 7.30pm (July–September)
• Tel: 91 510 84 64 / 91 510 84 69
• Metro: La Elipa
• Bus: 15, 28, 106, 110, 113, 210

Free-masonry's Eternal Orient

Inside the main entrance to Nuestra Señora de la Almudena cemetery, to the right, can be found the monumental tombs of some celebrated Freemasons.

Antonio Rodríguez García-Vao (1862–1886), journalist, poet and Republican writer. He was an activist in the Spanish Grand Orient, Ancient and Accepted Scottish Rite, and was stabbed by an unknown on the night of 18 December 1866, dying a few hours later. Many Freemasons, Republicans, intellectuals and artists attended his funeral, presided over by Spanish statesman Nicolás Salmerón (see below). Following a public subscription a mausoleum in his honour was erected over the tomb: first on the right through the main entrance. The mausoleum is in the form of an obelisk with the image of the deceased on the front. In Freemasonry, an obelisk represents the "pointed stone" or "stone of perfection" of the Master Mason. On the monument can be seen a triangle and compass, symbols of the Great Architect of the Eternal Orient, where the soul of the dead Freemason will go.

The tomb of **Nicolás Salmerón Alonso** (1838–1908), third president of the Spanish Republic and known as the Master Mason, is impressive in its strangeness: two columns stand before a stone triangle representing the two main columns of the entrance to Solomon's Temple, where God as the Unity and the Trinity is revealed to the gathering of faithful Israelites. Built in 1915, this funerary monument bears the following epitaph: "Through the elevation of his thought, through his spirit of inflexible rectitude, through the noble dignity of his life, Nicolás Salmerón honoured his country and Humanity".

Nor does the grave of **Ramón Chíes,** who died at Madrid in 1894, pass unnoticed. Chíes was editor of *Las Dominicales de Libre Pensamiento*, a Masonic and Republican weekly journal. The memorial shows an inverted triangle, symbol of Masonic death, and on the upper part are represented the three Masonic degrees of Apprentice – Partner – Teacher and the supreme divinity known as the Great Architect of the Universe.

A little further on is another imposing grave: the mausoleum dedicated to **Francisco Pi y Margall** (1824–1901), executive president of the Spanish First Republic and an eminent Freemason. On the entrance portico of the mausoleum is the head of a winged angel representing the liberty and free thought that Pi y Margall defended until his dying day.

You'll find other graves in the cemetery for personalities who had links with Freemasonry, such as the celebrated broken column with the sculpture of the intertwined set-square and compasses, universal Masonic symbol. The link between the two takes the form of what is known as the "lake of love", i.e. love parting for the Eternal Orient, beyond death. The message of this anonymous tomb is perhaps the most significant in the cemetery.

The tomb of the **Serna Alonso Sanz San Miguel** family was commissioned by Freemason Francisco Sanz, who is laid to rest there. The front shows a Masonic triangle where you can read the following epitaph: "*Sonreídme, que voy a donde estáis vosotros, los de siempre*"("Smile on me, I am going there where you are, you my friends always").

In the discreet grave of **Antonia Rubio**, Freemason of the Rite of Adoption (for women), can also be seen the intertwined set-square and compasses leaning towards acacia leaves, which in Masonic symbolism represent initiation and immortality.

Finally, without mentioning all worth seeing, are the tombs of Julián Sanz del Río (1869), Fernando de Castro (1874), Pablo Iglesias (1925) and Julián Basterio (1940).

The cemetery was constructed almost a century and a half after the appearance, in 1728, of the first lodge in Spain, founded in Madrid by Philip, Duke of Wharton, ex-Grand Master of the Grand Lodge of England.

ALMOND BLOSSOM IN QUINTA DE LOS MOLINOS

La Quinta de los Molinos
Miami, 5 and Alcalá, 527
• Second and third week in March
• Open daily from 6.30am to 10pm
• Metro: Suances

A s winter draws to a close Quinta de los Molinos park offers a magnificent natural spectacle: during the second and third weeks of March the blossoming of over a thousand almond trees covers everything with a pink and white mantle, just like a Japanese print.

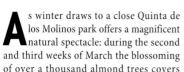

*A park
unique
of its kind*

Besides the almond trees that make Quinta de los Molinos park unique, you can also stroll among dozens of olives, birch, seringat (mock orange), eucalyptus, mimosa and large bushy shrubs which give the place a wild air. All along the paths and tracks that criss-cross the park's 25 hectares, can be seen ivys, petunias, privets, lilies and an infinite variety of flowers and shrubs. To the north is the Casa del Reloj ("Clock House"), where gardening courses used to be held, and a mansion built in 1925 that resembles a Viennese palace.

The name of the park comes from the two windmills that can still be seen near the mansion. They are the outward parts of a complex irrigation system with its origins in the wells and springs discovered during the construction of the property. To store and distribute the water, several ponds, tanks and fountains were created, at once fulfilling an ornamental role.

La Quinta de los Molinos belonged to the Count of Torre Arias who, at the beginning of the twentieth century, gifted it to the architect of Alicante, César Cort Boti, professor of town planning at the School of Architecture and a city councillor. Cort acquired the surrounding properties and ended up owning some 30 hectares of land, where he had a vast Mediterranean-style park laid out. Around 1982, Cort's heirs came to an agreement with the municipal planning services and handed over three-quarters of the property to the city hall. The remainder, more or less 5 hectares of treeless land, was used for a housing project. Thanks to this arrangement the park was opened to the public and now it's a real privilege to be able to stroll around in a semi-deserted oasis of greenery.

TRACES OF THE CIVIL WAR IN EL CAPRICHO PARK ⑲

Alameda de Osuna s/n
• Open Saturday, Sunday and public holidays from 9am to 6.30pm
(1 October–31 March); Saturday, Sunday and public holidays from 9am
to 9pm (1 April to 30 September)
• Metro: El Capricho

> **Bunker with ammunition store ...**

El Capricho (The Caprice) is the finest romantic park in the city, perhaps the reason why cycles, pet animals and picnics are banned.

The park was commissioned by Doña María Josefa Alonso Pimentel, Duchess of Osuna, at the end of the eighteenth century. She wished to have a place where she could indulge her taste for contemporary trends. So she had an elegant mansion built surrounded by gardens where every minute detail was carefully attended to: from a labyrinth of shrubbery and an exedra (walled recess with raised seating) housing sphinxes to the little Greek temple dedicated to Dionysus.

The park has also known some difficult times, as when the French army used its buildings as soldiers' barracks during the War of Independence at the beginning of the nineteenth century. Once the war was over and the park returned to the hands of its proper owners, the years rolled by uneventfully, far from the sumptuous receptions that the duchess used to organise. It was only in the 1930s under the Second Republic that the park was designated a Historic Garden, although shortly afterwards it became a strategic site for the defence of the capital during the Civil War.

During the war General José Miaja set up the barracks from which he directed the defence of Madrid. Under threat of invasion by the rebel troops, the High Command of the Central Army of the Republic moved into the bunker that the general had had prepared, and where later the surrender of Madrid was decided.

The generously sized bunker is beside the little mansion, while at the entrance stands the ammunition dump that supplied a great many of the troops. Today these buildings are closed to the public although if you visit the park you can see the entrance doors and the basement windows.

In the 1960s, the park was one of the locations for David Lean's film *Doctor Zhivago*.

HERMIT FORBIDDEN TO CUT HIS HAIR ...
The Duchess of Osuna also had built a landing stage and a hermitage for which she engaged a hermit whom she forbade to cut his hair, according to rumours of the time.

CALLE MARIO ROSO DE LUNA

• Metro: El Capricho

Magus in the city

Not far from Madrid's avenue de los Ingenieros Hermanos Granda is a street bearing the name of Mario Roso de Luna in homage to the greatest doyen of the Masonic tradition that the Iberian Peninsula has known in the past few centuries. Mario Roso de Luna was born on 15 March 1872 at Logrosán (Extremadura) and died on 8 November 1931. A man of letters and a scientist, follower of spiritualist philosophy, he was also an astronomer, journalist, writer and theosopher. All these reasons led Madrid to pay him homage by naming a street after him. From childhood, Mario Roso de Luna proved to be a prodigy with advanced intellectual abilities. At the age of 18 he obtained his law degree and was awarded a doctorate in 1894 when he was 22. In 1901, he graduated in physics and chemistry. He had also shown a keen interest in astronomy and in 1893, aged 21, he discovered a comet that has since been named after him. Known as the *Mago Rojo de l'Auto-Réalisation* ("Red Magus of Self-Determination") Roso de Luna liked to define himself as a "theosopher and Athenaeum member". He was in fact a leading member of the Ateneo Científico y Literario (Scientific and Literary Athenaeum, see p. 134). A notable characteristic of this Madrilene institution was that between the late nineteenth and the early twentieth centuries so many Masonic and theosophical meetings were held there that it was generally thought of as Madrid's Theosophical School. It was there that Mario Roso de Luna first came into contact with Freemasonry. He was initiated at Seville on 8 January 1917 in the Lodge of Isis and Osiris, whose Grand Master was Diego Martínez Barrio. Around this time Roso de Luna adopted the symbolic name of "*Prisciliano*". In this way he formed a connection with the Spanish Grand Orient (federation of lodges) and, under the authority of the Spanish Symbolic Grand Lodge of the Rite of Memphis and Mizraim, the following year he founded at Miajadas, not far from his birthplace, the Lodge of the Symbolic Rite in which he managed to attain the 33rd grade. At the time, most Freemasons in Madrid and Extremadura were also theosophists belonging to the Theosophical Society co-founded by Madame Helena Blavatsky in the nineteenth century. Mario Roso de Luna had been a member through a theosophical league in London well before he became a Freemason. He was also a tireless traveller and in his capacity as a theosopher disseminated vast quantities of information. He translated the works of Helena Blavatsky into Spanish and wrote a number of books collected in what is known as the *Biblioteca de las Maravillas (Library of Marvels)*. Roso de Luna's work applied the theosophical doctrine to a great variety of subjects, such as musicology ("Beethoven, theosopher"; "Wagner, mythologist and occultist"), sexology ("Psychic aberrations of sex"), Arab mythology ("The thousand and one nights – the veil of Isis"), pre-Columbian myths ("Hieratic science of the Maya"), Spanish folklore ("The book that kills Death") and even totalitarianism ("Humanity and the Caesars"). Thus he showed his anti-militarism and his revulsion for all forms of religious or secular dictatorships, and confirmed his interest in social problems, as borne out in 1905 when he carried through a model school project for the education and training of children with problems. Mario Roso de Luna left a wide-ranging and prolific body of work published in the contemporary press in his capacity as newspaper and book contributor. Thus he spread not only the spiritual ideas of modern humanity but also threw light on the recent scientific and technological discoveries, aiming to promote individual fulfilment and social progress. In 1910, he travelled to South America and gave a series of theosophical conferences which were a resounding success. In Brazil, where he found himself at the beginning of 1911, the founder of the Brazilian Theosophical Society, Professor Henrique José de Souza, acclaimed him as the greatest thinker of the twentieth century. In the Brazilian city of São Lourenço de Minas Gerais do Sul there is an avenue bearing the name of Mario Roso de Luna in memory of the *Mago de Logrosán*. Spain also paid tribute to the man and his body of work. As well as calle de Mario Roso de Luna in Madrid, there is also an Institute of Mario Roso de Luna Studies at Logrosán. A street in Cáceres and another in Mérida are also named after him.

EXORCIST OF NUESTRA SEÑORA DE ZULEMA PARISH

㉑

Alcalá de Henares
• www.fortea.ws

> *Exorcism is alive and well in Madrid*

In a city with one monument dedicated to Lucifer (see p. 35) and another to Faust (p. 231), where ghost stories are ubiquitous (p. 110 and p. 113), and where a legend tells of how the devil hid a French captain in a bell-tower near Puerta del Sol (p. 127), the presence of an exorcist is hardly surprising.

José Antonio Fortea is the only exorcist officially practising in Spain. The priest, who lives a half-hour's drive from Madrid at Alcalá de Henares, regularly meets people thought to be possessed by demons besides offering the traditional Mass.

According to Father Fortea, possessed people show the following characteristics: they dribble white spittle, fall into a trance, blaspheme and use dead languages, bark like a dog and show physical aversion to the word "God" or any religious object.

Roman Catholic tradition has it that possession was originally linked to practices such as spiritualism (for example making tables spin), or to the Cuban *Santería*.* Practices that did not demand the invocation of spirits, such as tarot reading, are not a demonic risk, even if they are banned.

Many of the cases treated by Father Fortea are not strictly speaking considered to be possessed, but rather to be suffering from psychotic impulsions such as paranoid schizophrenia or anxiety attacks.

The priest knows that he has a demon to deal with if any form of prayer is rejected. When this happens, before going any further, he holds a long conversation with the person concerned in which he exhaustively analyses the situation to determine if it is in fact demonic possession or a psychiatric case.

The exorcism rite takes place in a church, in the presence of the family and friends of the possessed person. Father Fortea says prayers to ward off the demon and beseeches it to leave the person's body. The number of sessions required varies.

Father Fortea, who has written a thesis on exorcism, is authorised by the Vatican to put his knowledge into practice. He is also the author of numerous books on the subject, the most recent being *Memorias de un exorcista* in which he gives an account of the vicissitudes of a priest who has committed himself to fighting the devil.

Santería (Way of the Saints): religious tradition of African Yoruba and Catholic origin that developed in Cuba.

DON JUSTO CATHEDRAL

Calle del Arquitecto Antonio Gaudí, 2
Mejorada del Campo
• Bus 282 from Avenida de América station below Avenida de América metro

A cathedral constructed from recycled materials

One of the most unusual cathedrals in the world is located, quite coincidentally, in calle del Arquitecto Antonio Gaudí, at Mejorada del Campo. This curious monument is the work of octogenarian Justo Gallego Martínez who for the best part of half a century has expended all his energy on this original temple, which he has built single-handed with recycled materials.

Don Justo, who in his youth had to abandon his religious vocation because of tuberculosis, decided in 1961 to devote his life to building this cathedral dedicated to Nuestra Señora del Pilar (Our Lady of the Pillar, the name given to the Virgin Mary on her appearance in Spain). So the self-taught architect, after meticulous labour that nobody took seriously at first, created the astonishing structure that can be seen today on land inherited from his parents, without planning permission, any institutional assistance or help from the Church.

At first he financed his project by selling his possessions, but over time donations began to come in. Nor had Don Justo drawn up any plans (it was all in his head) so in order to compensate for his lack of specialist training, he found inspiration by consulting books on châteaux and cathedrals.

The recycled materials are of all kinds, such as the bicycle wheel that he uses as a pulley and, rising among the irregular galleries and spiral staircases are columns formed from chemical containers and arches based on lorry tyres.

Don Justo estimates that it will take him another fifteen years to finish his work, but the edifice that at first seemed like a folly now has a cupola 11 metres in diameter and 40 metres high. Inside, a pile of old school chairs waits for Mass to begin.

AHORA QUE YA NO PUEDO SERTE UTIL
NI OBEDECERTE MAS
NI DARTE COMPAÑA
DESPUES DE QUE TE ENTREGUE TODA MI VIDA
DEMUESTRA QUE TU TAMBIEN FUISTE MI AMIGO
Martín Vigil

EL ÚLTIMO PARQUE

Antigua Ctra. Valencia Km. 30,400
Calle Aviación Espanola, 5 - Arganda del Rey
• Tel: 91 459 00 00 • Winter opening times: Saturday from 10am to 2pm
and 3.30pm to 6pm; Sunday from 10am to 2pm • Summer: Saturday from
10am to 2pm and 4.30pm to 7.30pm; Sunday from 10am to 2pm

*Pet
cemetery*

Although Egyptian tradition required that you shave your eyebrows when your cat died as a sign of mourning, in Madrid, the Último Parque (Last Park) offers to bury pet animals in an Italian marble tomb, with all the dignity befitting a human being.

The cemetery is set in pinewoods, far from the noise of the city, in a truly peaceful environment. Dogs, cats and even monkeys are buried there: in all, there are 4,000 pets' graves whose inscriptions and eccentric ornaments are different to those you can see in traditional cemeteries. Heroic animals are laid to rest here, such as the Yorkshire terrier accidently shot in his owner's arms, or the bitch that had given birth to over 200 puppies. When walking in this extensive park and reading the epitaphs and ornaments on the graves, you can guess the attachment between owners and pets. Some even leave bottles of water so their pets won't be thirsty in the afterlife!

Since 1983, El Ultimo Parque has also offered to collect your pet from wherever it has died and to organise the burial (there is also a cremation service).

You can choose from various marble or granite tombstones, with different typestyles for the inscription. Some particularly sumptuous tombs ("honour" model) are found in the most popular part of the cemetery. They are embellished with magnificent tombstones bearing the animal's name and an epitaph recalling its time on Earth. The less well-off can choose more modest graves. One of the advantages of this pet cemetery is that it guarantees a perpetual concession: an annual subscription means you don't have to worry about what will become of the grave in the future.

The price of a grave and burial ranges from €300 to €4,000.

There is also a dog cemetery at Asnières, near Paris (see *Banlieue de Paris insolite et secrète* in this series of guides) and another in Hyde Park (see *Secret London: An Unusual Guide*).

The Palacio de Liria (see p. 63) also has a small private cemetery for the Duchess of Alba's dogs and parrots.

ALPHABETICAL INDEX

ALPHABETICAL INDEX

THEMATIC INDEX

ARCHITECTURE

CHILDREN

CURIOSITIES

THEMATIC INDEX

ESOTERICISM

GARDENS - NATURE

HISTORY

THEMATIC INDEX

LIBRARIES

MUSEUMS

RELIGION

SCIENCES

Photography Credits

All photos were taken by **Manuel Vázquez** with the exception of:

María Antón: pages 29, 235.
Cristina Hidalgo: page 77.
Thomas Jonglez: pages 63, 133, 134, 137, 153, 163.
Carol Martínez: page 237.
Chino Miguel: pages 61, 65, 143, 155, 185.
Erik Mólgora: pages 19, 31, 51, 57, 95, 99, 103, 105, 109, 125, 127, 167, 169, 205, 212, 231.
Camilo Ospina: page 241.
Sergio Padura: page 203.
Ida Plaza: page 47.
Mali Ramírez: pages 119, 165, 175.
Lucrecia Salgari: pages 23, 33, 43, 67, 93, 141, 189, 199, 214, 217.
Manuel Villate: pages 83, 115.

The following photos have been graciously provided by:
Page 21: Fundación Carlos de Amberes
Page 24: Biblioteca Nacional de España
Page 54: Museo de la Farmacia Hispana
Page 75: Asociación Grama
Page 85: Salvemos el Frontón Beti-jai
Page 89 and 91: Emanuela Gambini
Page 116: Congreso de los Diputados
Page 121: El Deseo Producciones
Page 123: Joyería Grassy
Page 139: Ateneo de Madrid
Page 201: Fundación Infante de Orleáns. Javier Guerrero and Ismael Abeytua.

The following texts were written by:

Vitor Manuel Adrião: pages 26, 35, 37, 69, 113, 127, 128, 134, 144, 171, 173, 186, 207, 215, 218, 231, 232, 238.

Milí Crespo: pages 17, 91 and 229.

Carol Martínez: page 237.

Natalia Pianzola: pages 21, 41, 49, 53, 54, 55, 71, 81, 169, 211, 227, 243.

Acknowledgements: María Antón, Cristina Aranda, Ciro Arbós, Manuel Ayllón, Comandante Gabriel Balaguer Cortés, Fiorella Battistini, Carpetania Madrid, Manuel Bauer, José Bonifacio Bermejo, Yago Carrasco, Cristina Colmenar, Instituto Cervantes, Milí Crespo, Marina Díaz, Giselle Etcheverry, Óscar Fernández, Emanuela Gambini, Nabila Giha, Nicolás Giha, Mercedes Gómez, Juan Carlos González Morales, Miguel González, Rosa González Cebrián, Igor González Martín, Álvaro Hacar, Alfonso Herrán, Gonso Lara, Pilar Magnet, Beatrice Marcus, Ana Martín, Carolina Martínez, Eugenia Mazuecos, Ismael Millán, Eric Mólgora, Marianela Muro, Félix Piñuela, Sergio Padura, Silvia Pérez López, Ida Plaza, Pilar Quiñónez, Mali Ramírez, Carmen Rodríguez, Paz Sufrategui, Comandante Enrique Tabanera, Celia Teves, Tevi de la Torre, Morgana Vargas Llosa, Cristina Vázquez, Manuel Vázquez, Manuel Villate, Diana Wolfenzon.

Maps: **Cyrille Suss** - Layout Design: **Roland Deloi** - Layout: **Stéphanie Benoit** - English Translation: **Jeremy Scott, Kimberly Bess and Caroline Lawrence** - English Editing: **Kimberley Bess and Caroline Lawrence**

© JONGLEZ 2011
Registration of copyright: May 2011 – Edition: 01
ISBN: 978-2-9158-0767-7
Printed in France by Mame - 37000 Tours